THE ULTIMATE
CHICAGO WHITE SOX
TRIVIA BOOK

A Collection of Amazing Trivia Quizzes
and Fun Facts for Die-Hard White Sox Fans!

Ray Walker

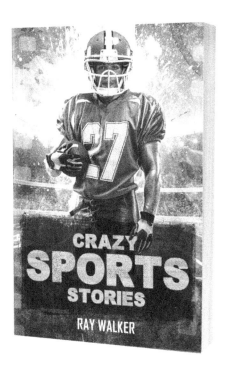

CONTENTS

INTRODUCTION

Obviously, you're inspired by your favorite team. In this case, the team in lights is none other than the Chicago White Sox. One of the original franchises in the American League, and surely one of the best ever in the entire glorious history of Major League Baseball (although archrival Minnesota Twins fans might want to argue over your claim just a bit).

Chicago, also known as "the Windy City", has always been filled with winning pro teams: the Chicago Bulls in the NBA, the Bears in the NFL, the MLS' Chicago Fire, the NHL's Blackhawks and the cross-town rival Cubs in Wrigley Field trying to hog the limelight. Giant corporations like Boeing, Caterpillar, United Airlines and Walgreens Boots make the city even more dynamic.

But your Chicago White Sox are extra special. There's no place in the world to play hardball like their unique home stadium located on Chicago's South Side, the new Comiskey Park, none other than Guaranteed Rate Field, filled with 40,615 screaming White Sox fans.

In 2021, the ChiSox will celebrate 120 years of existence at, or near, the peak of the baseball world. You'll be there for the celebration, armed with all the trivia and fun facts on their colorful players, big signings and trades, and the incredible emotional highs and lows of a world championship team. The White Sox have had more than their fair share of low times, and not just the team's tough postseason losses in 2000 and 2008. But we all must overcome, and there are many more merrier moments like the last World Series win in 2005.

Clearly you may use the book as you wish. Each chapter contains twenty quiz questions that are a mix of multiple choice, true or false formats, an answer key (don't worry, it's on a separate page!), and a section of ten "Did You Know?" factoids about the team.

And for the record, the information and stats in this book are current up to the beginning of 2020. The White Sox will surely break more records and win many more awards as the seasons march on, so keep this in mind when you're watching the next game with your friends. You never quite know: someone could suddenly start a conversation with the phrase "Did you know…?" And you'll be ready.

CHAPTER 1:

ORIGINS & HISTORY

QUIZ TIME!

1. How many World Series titles have the White Sox, also called the "South Siders", won in their history?

   a. 2
   b. 3
   c. 4
   d. 6

2. Which Midwestern city was responsible for the franchise's first name?

   a. Fargo, ND
   b. Omaha, NE
   c. Sioux City, IA
   d. Sioux Falls, SD

3. The team moved from St. Paul, Minn., to Chicago in 1900. The renamed American League achieved major-league status the next year with Chicago taking its first title in 1901.

a. True

b. False

4. What was the team's name until 1904?

   a. Black Stockings

   b. Illinois Fighting Illini

   c. Meat Packers

   d. White Stockings

5. The White Sox were forever tarnished by their involvement in "fixing" the 1919 World Series, thus earning the Black Sox moniker. Who was their opponent?

   a. Cincinnati Reds

   b. Detroit Tigers

   c. New York Giants

   d. Pittsburgh Pirates

6. Which of the following players was not on the list of those allegedly bribed to lose the 1919 World Series?

   a. Garland Braxton

   b. Oscar "Happy" Felsch

   c. "Shoeless Joe" Jackson

   d. George "Buck" Weaver

7. The 1919 White Sox clubhouse was apparently divided into two factions. What was the nickname of the "straight-laced" group who wouldn't accept bets?

   a. "Clean Sox"

   b. "Ivy League Sox"

   c. "No-Bet Ballplayers"

   d. "Whitest Sox"

8. Besides Chick Gandil, the mastermind of the fixed World Series, how much did the other players in the scandal each receive from gamblers?

   a. $2,500
   b. $5,000
   c. $10,000
   d. $25,000

9. Who was baseball's first commissioner responsible for banning the Series-fixing players for life?

   a. Happy Chandler
   b. Ford Frick
   c. Judge Kenesaw Mountain Landis
   d. Fay Vincent

10. After the scandal blew over, for how many years did the White Sox flounder before winning another pennant?

   a. 20
   b. 30
   c. 40
   d. 50

11. Following the long pennant drought, what was the nickname of the team that captured the next AL flag for Chicago?

   a. "Go-Go Sox"
   b. "No-Bull sox"
   c. "Sprinting Sox"
   d. "Winningest White Sox"

12. After the pennant-clinching drive that year, who was the Chicago mayor who ordered the city's air raid sirens to blow (confusing many Chicagoans at the height of the Cold War)?

    a. Anton Cermak

    b. Richard Daley

    c. Rahm Emanuel

    d. William Thompson

13. From their inception in 1901 to 2019, what's the White Sox winning percentage been?

    a. .502

    b. .515

    c. .533

    d. .545

14. What was the nickname of star shortstop Luke Appling who helped Chicago stay in the top half of the AL from 1936 to 1946?

    a. "Appling Tree"

    b. "Lightning Luke"

    c. "Never-Lose Luke"

    d. "Ol' Aches and Pains"

15. Starting in 1951, for how many consecutive seasons did the White Sox maintain a winning record?

    a. 13

    b. 15

    c. 17

    d. 21

16. When Bill Veeck and his group purchased a majority share in the club in 1958, what was one of the promotional stunts he pulled to draw more fans?

    a. Exploding scoreboard
    b. Free peanuts
    c. Half-naked cheerleaders
    d. Seventh inning stretch rock show

17. Which player who won the MVP with the White Sox in 1972 is sometimes given credit for keeping the team in Chicago?

    a. Dick Allen
    b. Catfish Hunter
    c. Sparky Lyle
    d. Joe Rudi

18. On July 12, 1979, an ill-fated promotion called "Disco Demolition Night" led to a riot and a damaged field. Who did the White Sox forfeit the second doubleheader game to as a result?

    a. Boston
    b. Cleveland
    c. Detroit
    d. Seattle

19. Which manager spearheaded Chicago's drive to the division title under new ownership in 1983?

    a. Pat Corrales
    b. Ralph Houk
    c. Tony La Russa
    d. Doug Rader

20. Which White Sox slugger who became the all-time club leader in doubles, HRs, and runs, turned into the face of the franchise in the '90s and early 2000s?

    a. Harold Baines

    b. Paul Konerko

    c. Greg Luzinski

    d. Frank Thomas

QUIZ ANSWERS

1. B - 3

2. C - Sioux City, IA

3. A - True

4. D - White Stockings

5. A - Cincinnati Reds

6. A - Garland Braxton

7. A - "Clean Sox"

8. B - $5,000 (equivalent to $74,000 in 2019)

9. C - Judge Kenesaw Mountain Landis

10. C - 40

11. A - "Go-Go Sox"

12. B - Richard Daley

13. A - .502

14. D - "Ol' Aches and Pains"

15. C - 17

16. A - Exploding scoreboard

17. A - Dick Allen

18. C - Detroit

19. C - Tony La Russa

20. D - Frank Thomas

DID YOU KNOW?

1. It only took a short time for Chicago scorekeeper Christoph Hynes to tire of writing out "White Stockings". He wrote "White Sox" on the scorecard in the early 1900s, and the name stuck.

2. The early White Sox were built on defense and pitching, especially behind "Big Ed" Walsh who pitched 400+ innings a year from 1907 and 1908.

3. The first time the Sox stole the World Series from the heavily favored Cubs was 1906. Due to their anemic team batting average, the White Sox team at the time was called "The Hitless Wonders".

4. Chicago hasn't always been the "friendliest" climate to play ball in: Opening Day on April 18, 1907, was the coldest ever at 38 degrees Farenheit (3.3 Celsius).

5. When Chicago blasted through the AL on their way to the 1917 Series, they went 100-54—still a franchise record for wins and winning percentage.

6. Eddie Collins was the big batter (.409) as the White Sox nipped the New York Giants to win the 1917 World Series, 4-2. Eddie Cicotte and Red Faber pitched 50 of 52 innings to dominate the mound.

7. One reason given for players taking bribes to fix the 1919 Series in the Black Sox Scandal was their dislike of Sox owner Charles Comiskey and his alleged stinginess.

8. In that sad World Series, Chicago's Lefty Williams lost the three games he pitched, a record for the Fall Classic.

9. During the so-called lean years from 1921 to 1936, Chicago almost landed Babe Ruth, but the Yankees secured the Bambino with more cash.

10. After Charles Comiskey died in 1931, his family continued to operate the franchise. First son Lou, then Louis' widow Grace, and finally their daughter, Dorothy Rigney, took the reins.

CHAPTER 2:

WHAT'S IN A NAME?

QUIZ TIME!

1. When the White Stockings won their first AL pennant in 1900, they were led by player-manager Dick Padden. What was his nickname?

    a. Balls

    b. Bats

    c. Brains

    d. Brawn

2. Clarence "Pants" Rowland became White Sox manager in 1915. He got his nickname from his base-running antics wearing his dad's overalls for the Ninth Street Blues team. From what city?

    a. Dubuque, Iowa

    b. Joliet, Illinois

    c. Peoria, Illinois

    d. Waterloo, Iowa

3. Who succeeded Pants as the White Sox manager in 1918?

    a. Dizzy Dean
    b. Kid Gleason
    c. Will Harridge
    d. Reb Russell

4. Shoeless Joe Jackson was born the son of a sharecropper in Pickens County, SC. Which disease almost killed him when he was 10?

    a. Malaria
    b. Measles
    c. Mumps
    d. Scarlet fever

5. Due to a lack of education, Shoeless Joe Jackson often had his wife sign things for him, thus inflating the value of his real signature. How much did one of his autographs sell for in 1990?

    a. $15,000
    b. $23,100
    c. $28,000
    d. $42,750

6. When Shoeless Joe Jackson and the "Eight Men Out" were convicted in the Black Sox Scandal, what was the famous 1921 headline that accompanied the trial?

    a. "Black Sox blacken baseball"
    b. "Joe, please say no."
    c. "Say it ain't so, Joe."
    d. "Shoeless and penniless too"

7. Drafted by Chicago in 1925, Leonardo "Leo Najo" Alanis was one of the first Mexican players to make it north of the border. Which team did he break in with?

    a. Amarillo Sod Poodles
    b. El Paso Diablos
    c. San Antonio Bears
    d. Shreveport Captains

8. Who was the White Sox's first black player in 1951?

    a. Willard "Home Run" Brown
    b. Willie Mays
    c. Minnie Miñoso
    d. Bob Trice

9. Which pair of brothers did Bill Veeck sell the team to because of his health problems?

    a. Arthur / John Allyn
    b. Arthur / Johnnie Ashe
    c. Frank / Jessie James
    d. Dick / Jerry Van Dyke

10. Which of the following White Sox player was NOT banned for life by Commissioner Landis due to the Black Sox Scandal?

    a. Babe Borton
    b. Charles "Swede" Risberg
    c. George "Buck" Weaver
    d. Claude "Lefty" Williams

11. Who played Buck Weaver in the 1988 film "Eight Men Out" directed by John Sayles?

    a. John Cusack
    b. Dustin Hoffman
    c. Kevin Kline
    d. Robert Redford

12. Which White Sox hurler won the Cy Young in 1959 when there was only one award for both leagues?

    a. Barry Latman
    b. Turk Lown
    c. Billy Pierce
    d. Early Wynn

13. Ted "Big Klu" Kluszewski was a key acquisition for the 1959 White Sox. What was the name of his nearby hometown?

    a. Argo, IL
    b. Goofy Ridge, IL
    c. Oblong, IL
    d. Ransom, IL

14. In the '59 World Series, Chicago took Game 5 off the Dodgers in the City of Angels in front of 92,706 fans—the largest crowd to ever witness a Series game. Who was the 23-year-old L.A. loser that day?

    a. Don Drysdale
    b. Carl Erskine
    c. Sandy Koufax
    d. Fernando Valenzuela

15. The 1977 version of the White Sox was affectionately known as the "South Side Hitmen". Which of the following players did NOT feature in that team?

    a. Harold Baines
    b. Oscar Gamble
    c. Eric Soderholm
    d. Richie Zisk

16. Which White Sox slugger was affectionately known as "the Big Hurt"?

    a. Jermaine Dye
    b. Ron Kittle
    c. Frank Thomas
    d. Robin Ventura

17. Which of the following minor league teams did Javier "The Silent Assassin" Vázquez NOT play with?

    a. Albany Polecats
    b. Delmarva Shorebirds
    c. Harrisburg Senators
    d. Winston-Salem Dash

18. Ken "Hawk" Harrelson spent 33 years covering all the excitement of White Sox baseball. What award did he win in 2020 for "major contributions to baseball"?

    a. Commissioner's Trophy
    b. Ford C. Frick Award
    c. Leo The Lip Announcing Award
    d. Vin Scully Locution Award

19. Which name did Ken Harrelson use to announce any play involving a broken bat?

    a. Carl Canofcorn
    b. Matt Abbatacola
    c. Matt Brokabatta
    d. Sherm Leftonbase Lollar

20. Manager Ozzie Guillén once said, "If you play against him, you hate him. If you play with him, you hate him a little less." Who was he referring to?

    a. A.J. Pierzynski
    b. José Contreras
    c. Scott Podsenik
    d. Juan Uribe

QUIZ ANSWERS

1. C - Brains

2. A - Dubuque, Iowa

3. B - Kid Gleason

4. B - Measles

5. B - $23,100

6. C - "Say it ain't so, Joe"

7. C - San Antonio Bears

8. C - Minnie Miñoso

9. A - Arthur / John Allyn

10. A - Babe Borton

11. A - John Cusack

12. D - Early Wynn

13. A - Argo, IL

14. C - Sandy Koufax

15. A - Harold Baines

16. C - Frank Thomas

17. D - Winston-Salem Dash

18. B - Ford C. Frick Award

19. B - Matt Abbatacola

20. A - A.J. Pierzynski

DID YOU KNOW?

1. Before A.J. Pierzynski played for Chicago, he was traded by the Twins to the Giants for Francisco Liriano, Joe Nathan and Boof Bonser.

2. MLB legend Ted "The Splendid Splinter" Williams called "Little Louie" Aparício "the best shortstop he'd ever seen". Louis helped the "Go-Go" White Sox win the 1959 AL pennant.

3. In 1966, Forrest "Smoky" Burgess set an MLB record for most games in a season (79) by a non-pitcher without scoring a run.

4. Eddie "Knuckles" Cicotte played minor league ball with the Augusta (GA.) Tourists alongside Ty Cobb in 1905.

5. Joe "Clutch Norris" Crede was a key Chicago cog when they won the 2005 Series, their first championship in 88 years.

6. When Carlton "Pudge" Fisk came to Chicago from Boston in 1981, he told the media, "After a decade with the Red Sox, it was time to change my sox!"

7. Jacob Nelson "Nellie" Fox was one of the best ever second basemen, and the third most difficult hitter to strike out in MLB history.

8. When "Goose" Gossage retired at the end of the 1987 season, he trailed only Rollie Fingers with 310 saves.

9. Vincent "Bo" Jackson is the only athlete ever to be named an All-Star in both pro baseball and football.

10. Theodore Amar Lyons, also known as "Sunday Teddy", is the only Hall of Fame pitcher to record more walks than strikeouts.

CHAPTER 3:

FAMOUS QUOTES

QUIZ TIME!

1. When Ted Lyons gave up a homer in Guam during WWII, he quipped, "I left the country to get away from _____ and here he is!" Who was the danger man?

   a. DiMaggio (Joe)

   b. Keller (Charlie)

   c. Mize (Johnny)

   d. Musial (Stan)

2. Which Sox manager said: "I told Roland (Hemond) to go out and get me a big-name pitcher. He said Wehrmeister's got 11 letters. Is that a big enough name for me?"

   a. Nixey Callahan

   b. Eddie Einhorn

   c. Clark Griffith

   d. Fielder Jones

3. What's missing from Eddie Cicotte's quote on his implication in the 1919 Black Sox Scandal? "I did it for _____."

a. all our great fans

b. everyone who's ever fought for money

c. the city of Chicago

d. the wife and kids

4. A ChiSox hurler affirmed, "A pitcher has to look at the hitter as his mortal enemy." Who was he?

a. Mark Buehrle

b. Billy "The Kid" Pierce

c. Ed Walsh

d. Early Wynn

5. "Bats don't like to freeze no more than me." Which player said this as he returned to his South Carolina home in winter?

a. Bill Melton

b. Carlos Lee

c. Jim Thome

d. Shoeless Joe Jackson

6. White Sox pitcher Robert Britt Burns claimed, "I think too much on the mound sometimes, and I get _____." What did he suffer from?

a. brain cramps

b. delusions

c. migraine headaches

d. social anxiety disorder

7. White Sox infielder Dick Allen once quipped, "If a horse can't eat it, then I don't like it." What material was he alluding to?

a. Artificial turf

b. Batting gloves

c. Metal bats

d. Sugar-free gum

8. When asked if he'd like to hit off a noted Chicago fireballer, manager Jeff Torborg retorted, "I'd rather catch him." Who was the speedballer?

   a. Freddy Garcia

   b. Goose Gossage

   c. Jack McDowell

   d. Sandy Consuegra

9. "I didn't realize it was big until our first year and we got our butts beat. I said, 'No, no, no, no—that can't happen anymore." What was manager Jerry Manuel referring to?

   a. Playing against the Cubs

   b. Playing against the Indians

   c. Playing against the Tigers

   d. Playing against the Twins

10. "Everybody says (Rod) Carew was the best left-handed hitter in the 1960s and '70s. But _____ could hit like Carew and he did it with power." Who was Bill Melton talking about?

    a. (Eddie) Collins

    b. (Roger) Maris

    c. (Joe) Morgan

    d. (Tony) Oliva

11. White Sox pitcher Early Wynn said, "I don't want any of those guys hitting the ball back at me. The mound is my _____ and I don't like my _____ being disturbed." Where did Wynn refer to?

  a. church
  b. home
  c. office
  d. sanctuary

12. In 1912, Shoeless Joe Jackson remarked, "What a hell of a league this is. I hit .387, .408, and .395 the last three years, and I ain't ____ nothing yet." What's missing?

  a. accomplished
  b. done
  c. hit
  d. won

13. "If you're cold, you can have a bad week in one day." Who was responsible for this cryptic quote about the damage to a player's psyche after going 0 for 8 in a doubleheader?

  a. José Abrea
  b. Luke Appling
  c. Tim Raines
  d. Greg Walker

14. "I could feel my adrenaline start to flow in about the sixth inning. I had to tell myself, "What the hell are you getting excited about? You're not going anywhere, big boy. Just go sign some autographs."" What was Goose Gossage talking about?

a. His first experiences as a bullpen coach
b. His first experiences as a general manager
c. His first experiences as a starting pitcher
d. Recovering from injury

15. What did Early Wynn quip when asked if he'd use brush-back tactics against his own mother?

    a. "My mom was never much of a hitter."
    b. "Not if I wanted any dinner."
    c. "Only if she were diggin' in."
    d. "Only if she were hittin' for the Cubs."

16. "Players come and go. It's the _____ you worry about. Without the _____, we wouldn't be here." What was Carlton "Pudge" Fisk referring to?

    a. fans
    b. field
    c. franchise
    d. game

17. "It looked like I was using a boxing glove down there. I think that hurt me a lot because it looked like the position was playing me." Which position did Herbert Perry make a lot of errors in during 2001 spring training?

    a. Catcher
    b. First base
    c. Shortstop
    d. Third base

18. After a thorough cross-examination in the 1919 Black Sox Scandal, Chicago manager William J. Gleason concluded, "I think they're the greatest ball club I've ever seen. Period." What was his nickname?

    a. Glee

    b. Kid

    c. The Wild One

    d. Wonderman

19. "It is the best bunch of fighters I ever saw. No game is lost until the last man is out. They can think for themselves which is still better." Who said this about the 1919 team just before they won the AL pennant?

    a. Gambler Aiden Clayton

    b. Mayor William Thompson

    c. Owner Charles Comiskey

    d. U.S. President Woodrow Wilson

20. "I started fouling off his pitches. I took a pitch every now and then. Pretty soon, after 24 fouls, old Red could hardly lift his arm and I walked. That's when they took him out of the game and he cussed me all the way to the dugout." Which Red was Luke Appling talking about in 1940?

    a. Adams / Cubs

    b. Faber / White Sox

    c. Ruffing / Yankees

    d. Schoendienst / Cards

QUIZ ANSWERS

1. A - DiMaggio (Joe)

2. B - Eddie Einhorn

3. D - the wife and kids

4. D - Early Wynn

5. D - Shoeless Joe Jackson

6. A - brain cramps

7. A - Artificial turf

8. B - Goose Gossage

9. A - Playing against the Cubs

10. D - (Tony) Oliva

11. C - office

12. D - won

13. D - Greg Walker

14. A - His first experiences as a bullpen coach

15. C - "Only if she were diggin' in."

16. D - game

17. D - Third base

18. B - Kid

19. C - Owner Charles Comiskey

20. C - Ruffing / Yankees

DID YOU KNOW?

1. When a couple of veteran managers talked about the joys of managing, Ozzie Guillen replied, "If this is the best job in baseball, then why do guys get gray hair and fat so quickly?"

2. Guillen talked about how hard it was to win respect in Chicago: "With 99 wins, we should get a little respect, a little love... But honestly, I kind of like not getting any. I was with a team a couple years ago that wasn't supposed to win one game, then all of a sudden won the world championship."

3. Finally, Guillen's take on the real value of his work: "It's a horse-(bleep) job. If you win, you get paid two million dollars. If you lose, you get fired."

4. Paul Konerko was never really known as a base stealer. He agreed, "Sure I steal bases. I just like to do it four at a time."

5. Jim Thome offered one reason why he bashed so many balls out of the park: "Having a little chip on your shoulder, a little arrogance with yourself. That's what I think is the little intangible that helps you win."

6. When manager Jeff Torborg was still in Cleveland, pitcher Jim Kern argued he should stay in the game as he wasn't tired. Torborg retorted, "I know Jim, but the outfielders are."

7. Announcer Ed Farmer described Mark Buehrle's speedy approach in finishing a game in less than two hours: "This guy's pitching like he's double-parked outside the facility here."

8. Shoeless Joe Jackson had a lot of fans, including fellow pitcher "Big Ed" Walsh: "Joe Jackson hit the ball harder than any man that ever played in the big leagues, and I don't except Babe Ruth."

9. White Sox catcher A.J. Pierzynski was quick to get the boot after an opposing batter walked and he said to the ump, "Give me a new ball. One you can see."

10. "There are murderers who serve a sentence and then get out. I got life," George Daniel "Buck" Weaver bemoaned his lifelong ban from baseball after the Black Sox Scandal.

CHAPTER 4:

WHITE SOX RECORDS

QUIZ TIME!

1. How many pennants have the White Sox won to go with their three World Championships?

    a. 4
    b. 6
    c. 8
    d. 9

2. Who was the longest-tenured White Sox manager with 1,850 games under his belt?

    a. Jimmy Dykes
    b. Ozzie Guillen
    c. Tony La Russa
    d. Les Moss

3. Which of the following players has NOT had his number retired by the White Sox?

    a. Luke Appling
    b. Carlton Fisk

   c. Frank Thomas

   d. Robin Ventura

4. Paul Konerko leads all White Sox in total bases with 4,010. Who comes in second with 3.949?

   a. Harold Baines

   b. Nellie Fox

   c. Minnie Miñoso

   d. Frank Thomas

5. Who tied Nellie Fox for most triples by a South Sider with 104?

   a. Shano Collins

   b. Lance Johnson

   c. Johnny Mostil

   d. Buck Weaver

6. In 1968, one White Sox pitcher appeared in no fewer than 88 games. Who was he?

   a. Eddie Fisher

   b. Bob Locker

   c. Damaso Marte

   d. Wilbur Wood

7. Who was the stingiest pitcher in terms of hits yielded per nine innings in White Sox history?

   a. Jack Harshman

   b. Juan Pizarro

   c. Chris Sale

   d. Hoyt Wilhelm

8. In his single season (2008) with Chicago, Orlando Cabrera racked up a single-season record of 661 at bats. Where was he born?

   a. Colombia

   b. Dominican Republic

   c. Puerto Rico

   d. Venezuela

9. Albert Belle blasted the ball in 1998. Which of the following single-season ChiSox records did he NOT set that year?

   a. Doubles

   b. Homers

   c. Runs

   d. Total Bases

10. Juan Pierre was the Chicago man for opponents to get out in 2010. He achieved that 530 times.

   a. True

   b. False

11. In 1956, Minnie Miñoso was hit by 23 pitches. Who tied that White Sox record in 2011?

   a. Gordon Beckham

   b. Eduardo Escobar

   c. Tyler Flowers

   d. Carlos Quentin

12. Which reliever piled up 57 saves, a single-season Chicago record, in 1990?

    a. Jerry Kutzler

    b. Donn Pall

    c. Scott Radinsky

    d. Bobby Thigpen

13. Patsy Flaherty's spitball didn't work as well for Chicago in 1903 as it did for the Boston Doves and Rustlers. What was the record number of losses he had that year?

    a. 23

    b. 25

    c. 28

    d. 32

14. Which White Sox hurler had the best strikeout-to-walk ratio in team history?

    a. Red Faber

    b. Ted Lyons

    c. Chris Sale

    d. Wilbur Wood

15. Which White Sox rookie set the record for most grand slams (4) by a first-year man in 2008?

    a. Jason Bourgeois

    b. Chris Getz

    c. Alexei Ramirez

    d. Clayton Richard

16. When the "South Side Hitmen" set an attendance record in 1977 (1,657,135 fans), who led the team in homers?

    a. Oscar Gamble

    b. Ralph Garr

c. Chet Lemon

d. Richie Zisk

17. The 1977 season was also the first year that the iconic song, "Na Na, Hey Hey (Kiss Him Goodbye)", was played. Who did the playing in Comiskey Park?

    a. Nancy Faust

    b. Mark Herman

    c. Al Melgard

    d. Gary Pressy

18. The White Sox didn't think too much about putting runs on the board against Kansas City on April 23, 1955. How many runs did they finally settle on?

    a. 22

    b. 26

    c. 29

    d. 33

19. Several Chicago players managed to steal four bags in a single game. Which of the following thieves did it three times?

    a. Jimmy Callahan

    b. George Davis

    c. Lou Frazier

    d. Scott Podsednik

20. The shortest game in AL history was a White Sox whitewashing of Philly, 5-0, on August 29, 1915. How long did Chicago take to put their opponents out of their misery?

a. 1:00
b. 1:08
c. 1:15
d. 1:25

QUIZ ANSWERS

1. B - 6

2. A - Jimmy Dykes

3. D - Robin Ventura

4. D - Frank Thomas

5. A - Shano Collins

6. D - Wilbur Wood

7. D - Hoyt Wilhelm (6.194)

8. A - Colombia

9. C - Runs

10. B - False / He achieved that 515 times.

11. D - Carlos Quentin

12. D - Bobby Thigpen

13. B - 25

14. C - Chris Sale / 4.69

15. C - Alexei Ramirez

16. A - Oscar Gamble (31 Homers)

17. A - Nancy Faust

18. C - 29

19. D - Scott Podsednik

20. B - 1:08

DID YOU KNOW?

1. Pat Seerey tied the AL record for total bases, amassing 16 in an 11-inning affair against Philly on July 18, 1948.

2. Several fearsome White Sox sluggers were given ample respect by opposing pitchers, all receiving five free passes in a single game: Frank Thomas, Jim Thome and Tony Muser.

3. Ozzie Guillén not only played for Chicago for 15 years, but he was the first Latino manager to guide his club to a World Series triumph (also the first for the White Sox in 88 years).

4. Guillen won AL Rookie of the Year in 1985 and became only the third rookie in MLB history to win a fielding title to boot.

5. When "the Hitless Wonders" copped the White Sox's first ever Series in 1906, Fielder Jones was the manager.

6. Although Luis Aparicio's number 11 jersey was retired, he requested its unique use for 11-time Gold Glove winner Omar Vizquel (also a Venezuelan).

7. Frank Thomas was voted by MLB fans as the franchise's "most outstanding player" in history for a combination of on-field performance, leadership, and quality of character.

8. Mark Buehrle's perfect game against Tampa Bay on July 23, 2009, earned him the Sporting News "Performance of

the Decade" (which went along with his other perfect game in April 2017).

9. 2007 saw the White Sox break all previous single-season attendance records by drawing 2,527,968 through the U.S. Cellular Field turnstiles.

10. Sammy Sosa played ball for the South Siders before becoming an infamous Cubbie. He was the youngest in franchise history at 21 years old to record 15 homers and 15 stolen bags (he finished with 32).

CHAPTER 5:

HOW ABOUT A TRADE?

QUIZ TIME!

1. Which player did Chicago receive from the Boston Red Sox for Tom Seaver in 1986?

   a. José DeLeón
   b. Richard Dotson
   c. Steve Lyons
   d. Gene Nelson

2. How many trades have the two Chicago teams pulled off in their illustrious histories?

   a. 20
   b. 26
   c. 42
   d. 64

3. Just before the 2017 Trade Deadline, which White Sox "workhorse" did the team send packing to the Cub in exchange for two prospects (Eloy Jimenez and Dylan Cease)?

a. Aaron Bummer

b. Tyler Clippard

c. Jace Fry

d. José Quintana

4. "If we really felt motivated to take an inferior baseball deal, to not put this organization in the best possible spot to win multiple championships simply because of emotion, then we would be the wrong people running this club." Who said this?

a. VP Moira Foy

b. GM Rick Hahn

c. Secretary Adam Klein

d. Chairman Jerry Reinsdorf

5. Which key pitching cog in 2005 did the White Sox get from the cross-town Cubs in 1998 for Matt Karchner?

a. Jim Abbott

b. Jon Garland

c. Jaime Navarro

d. Charlie O'Brien

6. On March 30, 1992, the White Sox acquired George Bell in exchange for Sammy Sosa and Ken Patterson. Why did Bell retire only two years later?

a. Back problems

b. Financial problems

c. Knee problems

d. Sciatic nerve pain

7. During his 12-year stint as White Sox GM, how many players did Ken Williams acquire?

    a. 123
    b. 147
    c. 171
    d. 212

8. Which player did the White Sox nab from the Mariners in 2004 to complete their 2005 World Series rotation?

    a. Ben Davis
    b. Freddy García
    c. Orlando Hernández
    d. Shingo Takatsu

9. Who did White Sox Chairman Jerry Reinsdorf once say was the only untouchable player he had trade-wise?

    a. Michael Jordan
    b. Paul Konerko
    c. Scottie Pippen
    d. Frank Thomas

10. The White Sox traded Chris Sale to Boston for a number of players in 2016. How many times did one of them, Yoán Moncada, fan in his first full Chicago year?

    a. 155
    b. 189
    c. 217
    d. 237

11. When Paul Konerko came to Chicago for Mike Cameron in late 1998, which of the following things did NOT happen?

    a. He hit 432 homers.

    b. He had 1,383 RBIs.

    c. He a concourse statue dedicated to him.

    d. He won three consecutive MVPs.

12. Which team traded the 1959 MVP second baseman Nellie Fox to Chicago in 1949?

    a. Baltimore Orioles

    b. Cleveland Indians

    c. Philadelphia A's

    d. Washington Senators

13. When Ken Williams and Ozzie Guillén traded for Scott Podsednik and Luis Vizcaino, what was the nickname given to the 2004 Minnesota Twins team the White Sox were trying to compete with?

    a. badgers

    b. gophers

    c. piranhas

    d. sharks

14. Which player was Chicago able to add through free agency with the money they saved in the aforementioned trade?

    a. Jermaine Dye

    b. Tadehito Iguchi

    c. Bobby Jenks

    d. Aaron Rowand

15. The White Sox gave up Esteban Loaiza to the Yankees in 2004 for José Contreras and cash. For what award had Loaiza been the AL runner-up just the previous year?

    a. Cy Young
    b. MVP
    c. Rookie of the Year
    d. Silver Slugger

16. When the White Sox traded with the Phillies for Jim Thome in 2005, besides Aaron Rowand and Daniel Haigwood, who was the so-called "player to be named later"?

    a. Roberto Alomar
    b. Gio González
    c. Miguel Olivo
    d. Wilson Valdez

17. Despite giving up Rowand, White Sox fans will forever remember Thome for his prodigious blast to beat the Twins, 1-0, in the 2008 AL Central Tiebreaker. What was the game nicknamed?

    a. The Blackout Game
    b. The (Nick Black-) Burnout Game
    c. The Thome Home Job
    d. The Twin Toaster

18. Which player has turned into a "superstar" for the Padres after being traded by Chicago in 2016?

    a. Tim Anderson
    b. Jabari Blash

c. James Shield

d. Fernando Tatis, Jr.

19. Besides making the Cubs a better team overall, how many homers did Sammy Sosa give the other Chicago team after his 1992 trade?

    a. 485

    b. 520

    c. 545

    d. 609

20. After his trade to Chicago, what was James Shields's won-loss record in 2.5 seasons?

    a. 10-41

    b. 16-35

    c. 25-26

    d. 27-24

QUIZ ANSWERS

1. C - Steve Lyons

2. B - 26

3. D - José Quintana

4. B - GM Rick Hahn

5. B - Jon Garland

6. C - Knee problems

7. C - 171

8. B - Freddy García

9. A - Michael Jordan

10. C - 217

11. D - He won three consecutive MVPs.

12. C - Philadelphia A's

13. C - piranhas

14. B - Tadehito Iguchi

15. A - Cy Young

16. B - Gio González

17. A - The Blackout Game

18. D - Fernando Tatis, Jr.

19. C - 545

20. B - 16-35

DID YOU KNOW?

1. Even though Todd Frazier cranked 40 home runs for Chicago in 2016 (joining only six other White Sox players with that number), he was quickly shipped to the Yankees the next season.

2. The White Sox almost landed a certain player named Babe Ruth when Boston owner Harry Frazee shopped the big man. The Yankees came up with the cash, and you know the rest.

3. With Chicago only 3.5 games behind Cleveland in 1995, Reinsdorf engineered the "White Flag Trade" sending three key players to San Fran for six minor leaguers.

4. Three years later, Chicago won the Central Division with significant contributions by two of the traded Giants, Ketih Foulke and Bob Howry.

5. By the end of 2002, none of the players secured by either team in the trade was playing for the team they were swapped to.

6. When Chicago traded for Nellie Fox in 1949, he was little known. The same wasn't true for trade bait Joe Tipton who had exchanged fisticuffs with manager Jack Onslow.

7. After Mike Cameron's trade to the Mariners, he "haunted" his former team with four dingers in one game. But Paul Konerko, acquired for Cameron, bashed a grand slam in Game 2 of the 2005 World Series.

8. Shoeless Joe Jackson arrived in Chicago in exchange for Larry Chappell, Ed Klepfer, Braggo Roth, and $31,500.

9. Despite batting .375, bashing a homer and six RBIs in the 1919 World Series, Jackson was banned from baseball in the Black Sox Scandal. Klepfer had a reasonable career, cut short by WWI.

10. José Contreras looked tough after winning 17 consecutive Yankee starts spanning 2005-06. Chicago coughed up Loaiza, who never found the same 2003 form again.

CHAPTER 6:

CHAT ABOUT STATS

QUIZ TIME!

1. According to baseball-reference.com, who was ranked as Chicago's best team batter in 2020?

    a. José Abreu
    b. Tim Anderson
    c. Yasmani Grandal
    d. Danny Mendick

2. What were the odds on the White Sox winning the Series in 2020, according to the same site?

    a. 1.5%
    b. 3.5%
    c. 7.25%
    d. 12%

3. What was the final score of the Chicago White Stockings' first ever game against an Illinois team (namely the University of Illinois) in 1900?

a. 15-14

b. 12-11

c. 10-9

d. 2-1

4. The 1906 White Sox team captured the pennant with an anemic .230 batting average and only seven homers. They went on to beat the Cubs 4-2 in the only all-Chicago Fall Classic ever.

a. True

b. False

5. Charles "The Old Roman" Comiskey looked west for the final piece to his 1917 Black Sox puzzle. Which third baseman did he snare from the PCL's Vernon (CA) Tigers?

a. Ziggy Hasbrook

b. Byrd Lynn

c. Charles "Swede" Risberg

d. Zeb Terry

6. When the newly expanded Comiskey Park opened on April 20, 1927, how many additional fans could squeeze in?

a. 10,500

b. 16,800

c. 23,200

d. 27,500

7. The first-ever All-Star Game was played in Chicago on July 6, 1933 and won by a two-run Babe Ruth blast. What event was the game part of?

a. Albert Einstein's U.S. Arrival
b. Baseball's Centennial Celebration
c. Franklin D. Roosevelt's Inauguration
d. World's Fair

8. Luke Appling, also known as "Old Aches and Pains", became a Hall of Famer in 1964. What was his AL-best batting average to win the 1936 batting title?

   a. .357
   b. .367
   c. .388
   d. .399

9. In the 1950 All-Star Game at Comiskey Park, the NL secured a dramatic 4-3 win on a Red Schoendienst homer (Ted Williams also broke his elbow). In what inning did Red go deep?

   a. 9th
   b. 11th
   c. 12th
   d. 14th

10. Among his numerous innovations, Bill Veeck attracted fans with fireworks, players' names on the back of uniforms, an exploding scoreboard and by hiring a midget player. Who was he?

    a. Earl Battey
    b. Walt Dropo
    c. Eddie Gaedel
    d. Stover McIlwain

11. When the White Sox wrested the pennant from the Indians in 1959, what was the team's combined ERA?

    a. 2.74
    b. 3.08
    c. 3.29
    d. 3.33

12. On the final day of the 1971 season, "Beltin'" Bill Melton copped the first-ever AL homer crown for a South Sider with his 33rd blast. Who was the opposing pitcher?

    a. Boston's Ken Brett
    b. Detroit's Mickey Lolich
    c. Milwaukee's Bill Parsons
    d. Oakland's Rollie Fingers

13. Despite winning 90 games and slugging a then-team-record 192 dingers, how many games behind the Royals did the White Sox end up in 1977?

    a. 8
    b. 10
    c. 12
    d. 13

14. When the impressive new Comiskey Park opened on April 18, 1991, how many rabid fans made Opening Day a sellout?

    a. 38,293
    b. 42,191
    c. 44,445
    d. 48,154

15. The 2002 White Sox regularly blasted the ball out of Comiskey and all other parks. Who did NOT belt at least 25 homers on the year?

    a. Royce Clayton
    b. Paul Konerko
    c. Carlos Lee
    d. Magglio Ordonez

16. On January 31, 2003, U.S. Cellular signed a 26-year naming rights deal with the White Sox. What was the accord worth?

    a. $46 million
    b. $55 million
    c. $68 million
    d. $80 million

17. A year later, Chicago's first Far Eastern import, Shingo Takatsu, saved 19 games. How many chances did he need?

    a. 20
    b. 25
    c. 28
    d. 33

18. Bobby Jenks juked the ball over the plate in Chicago in 2007, recording his second straight season of 40+ saves. How many consecutive outs did he rack up the same year?

    a. 36
    b. 42
    c. 47
    d. 52

19. 2011 saw Konerko clock 30 homers, 100 RBIs, and bat at least .300 for the second straight year. Which other White Sox player joined Konerko by earning their 2,000th career hit that season?

    a. Gordon Beckham
    b. Bibb Falk
    c. Juan Pierre
    d. Alex Rios

20. In 2015, Chris Sale blazed past Ed Walsh's single-season strikeout record of 269 set in 1908. What was the new mark?

    a. 274
    b. 280
    c. 292
    d. 301

QUIZ ANSWERS

1. C - Yasmani Grandal

2. B - 3.5%

3. C - 10-9

4. A - True

5. C - Charles "Swede" Risberg

6. C - 23,200

7. D - World's Fair

8. C - .388

9. D - 14th

10. C - Eddie Gaedel (1958)

11. C - 3.29

12. C - Milwaukee's Bill Parsons

13. C - 12

14. B - 42,191

15. A - Royce Clayton

16. C - $68 million

17. A - 20

18. B - 42

19. C - Juan Pierre

20. A - 274

DID YOU KNOW?

1. In 1979, at the height of disco fever, the White Sox held an infamous promo, "Disco Demolition Night", led by shock jock Steve Dahl and 97.9 WLUP.

2. Any fan who coughed up a vinyl disc was allowed to see a doubleheader between Chicago and Detroit for 98 cents, and to witness an explosion of the vinyl between games. In the end, fans stormed the field, and Chicago forfeited the second game.

3. Carlos May played in 1,002 games for the White Sox, hitting .275 in his tenure from 1968 to 1976. He's the only player in MLB history to wear his whole birthday on his uniform back: "May 17".

4. The 2005 version of the White Sox set the MLB standard by holding a lead in the season's first 37 games.

5. That magical 2005 season saw the White Sox join only four other teams in MLB annals to lead their division wire-to-wire and go on to cop the World Series.

6. Of those five teams: Chicago, the 1990 Reds, and the 1927 Yankees went on to sweep the Fall Classic.

7. It appears the 2005 White Sox did it all: they enjoyed three eight-game winning streaks before July 1 rolled around.

8. That indomitable Chicago squad was the first in MLB history to clinch all their postseason series on the road. The 2010 Giants and 2018 Red Sox have since done the same.

9. The 2005 team joined the 1999 Yankees as the only ones in MLB record books to suffer merely one postseason loss in a World Series run in the Wild Card era. Both teams went 11-1.

10. In August 2020, Lucas Giolito hurled the 19th White Sox no-no in franchise history—in the middle of a pandemic, in front of zero fans.

CHAPTER 7:

DRAFT DAY

QUIZ TIME!

1. Since the inception of the draft, how many first-round selections have the White Sox made?

    a. 50
    b. 60
    c. 74
    d. 80

2. For which position has the team never drafted a player in the first round?

    a. First base
    b. Second Base
    c. Shortstop
    d. Third base

3. Of the 34 pitchers Chicago has drafted, what's the ratio of right-handed to left-handed hurlers?

    a. 16:16
    b. 18:14

c. 22:12

d. 24:8

4. Which of the following states has NOT provided the White Sox with at least six first-round picks?

   a. California
   b. Florida
   c. Illinois
   d. Texas

5. Which of the following illustrious White Sox first-round selections made it all the way to the Hall?

   a. Harold Baines
   b. Jack McDowell
   c. Aaron Rowand
   d. Frank Thomas

6. Which of the following first-round picks has won a World Series championship with the team?

   a. Steve Buechele
   b. Danny Goodwin
   c. Aaron Rowand
   d. Bobby Seay

7. What prestigious award did 1987 first-round pick Jack McDowell haul in?

   a. Comeback Player of the Year
   b. Cy Young
   c. MVP
   d. Silver Slugger

8. The White Sox selected catcher Ken Plesha in the first round of the inaugural 1965 draft. What university did Ken attend?

   a. Northwestern
   b. Notre Dame
   c. University of Chicago
   d. University of Illinois

9. Outfielder Carlos May was selected in the first round by Chicago in 1966. After his MLB career, what Japanese team did Carlos grace?

   a. Chunichi Dragons
   b. Hanshin Tigers
   c. Nankai Hawks
   d. Yomiuri Giants

10. Brian Anderson was drafted in 2003 as an outfielder out of the University of Arizona. What position did he later convert to?

   a. Catcher
   b. First base
   c. Pinch hitter
   d. Pitcher

11. After being drafted in 2008, Gordon Beckham had two separate tours in Chicago. Which of the following teams did he NOT play for?

   a. Atlanta
   b. Detroit

c. New York Yankees

d. Seattle

12. Out of Lakeland, Florida, Chris Sale came to Chicago in the 2008 draft. How many times has the tall strikeout specialist been an All-Star?

a. 3

b. 5

c. 7

d. 9

13. Catcher Zack Collins cruised into Chicago in the 2016 draft. Which team had previously drafted him in 2013 but failed to sign Zachary?

a. Boston

b. Cincinnati

c. San Francisco

d. Seattle

14. Garrett Crochet was picked up by Chicago with the 11th pick of the 2020 draft. How much was his signing bonus?

a. $547,500

b. $1,677,000

c. $2,847,800

d. $4,547,500

15. Which star free agent did the White Sox lose in 2012 allowing them to pick up a supplemental first-round pick?

a. Dylan Axelrod

b. Mark Buehrle

c. Jake Peavy

d. Dayan Viciedo

16. For which player did the Yankees need to cough up a compensatory pick to the White Sox in 1983?

a. Don Baylor

b. Steve Kemp

c. Don Mattingly

d. Willie Randolph

17. Harold Baines not only collected 2,844 hits and 326 homers after being picked by the Sox in 1977, but he also coached on the 2005 champs. What high school was he drafted from?

a. DeSoto Central, Southhaven, Mississippi

b. Orange Lutheran, Orange, California

c. Spruce Creek, Port Orange, Floria

d. St. Michaels, Easton, Maryland

18. Robin Ventura was drafted out of Oklahoma State in 1988. With whom is he tied for fifth all-time in grand slam homers?

a. Lou Gehrig

b. Willie Mays

c. Willie McCovey

d. Eddie Murray

19. Jack "Black Jack" McDowell, picked out of Stanford in 1987, racked up 127 major-league wins in his career. What rock band did he also play for?

a. Devo

b. Steely Dan

c. Stickfigure

d. Sting

20. Alex Fernandez, drafted out of Miami-Dade in 1990, pitched six years for Chicago and won a Series with the Marlins. What trophy did he win as best college baseball player of the year?

a. Dick Howser Trophy

b. Hank Aaron Award

c. Hutch Award

d. Luis Aparicio Award

QUIZ ANSWERS

1. C - 74

2. B - Second base

3. C - 20:12

4. D - TX

5. D - Frank Thomas

6. C - Aaron Rowand

7. B - Cy Young

8. B - Notre Dame

9. C - Nankai Hawks

10. D - Pitcher

11. C - New York Yankees

12. C - 7

13. B - Cincinnati

14. D - $4,547,500

15. B - Mark Buehrle

16. B - Steve Kemp

17. D - St. Michaels, Easton, Maryland

18. C - Willie McCovey

19. C - Stickfigure

20. A - Dick Howser Award

DID YOU KNOW?

1. Alex Fernandez lost his no-hit bid against the Cubs at Wrigley on April 10, 1997, with one out in the ninth, allowing the ball to slide under his glove.

2. Aaron Rowand earned All-America honors at Cal State-Fullerton before being selected by the Sox as the 35th pick (first round) in 1998.

3. Ron Karkovice caught his entire career for Chicago after his draft in 1982. He earned the nickname "Officer Ron" from Ken Harrelson for his ability to throw out would-be base stealers.

4. Tim Anderson, taken by the Sox in the 2013 draft, didn't even play baseball until his junior year of high school due to injuries inflicted playing hoops.

5. Anderson was a bit of a base-stealing threat at East Central Community College in Decatur, MS, nabbing 30 in 30 attempts as a freshman. He stole 41 bases on 45 attempts the following season before being drafted by the Sox.

6. Frank Thomas's 1989 selection by Chicago looks awesome in hindsight: The only MLB player ever with seven straight seasons of at least a .300 batting average, 100 RBIs, 100 runs, 100 walks, and 20 dingers.

7. Despite Thomas's batting prowess, he was somehow not taken in the 1986 amateur draft. He headed off to Auburn to play some football.

8. When "The Big Hurt" bashed his 500th homer, he said, "It means a lot to me because I did it the right way,"hinting at Barry Bonds' steroid-fueled pursuit of Hank Aaron's homer mark.

9. White Sox draftee Robin Ventura fashioned a record 58-game hitting streak as an Oklahoma State Cowboy. He also managed the Sox for five seasons.

10. Drafted 10th by the Sox, Robin's pro start was tough with a 0-for-41 slump and 25 errors. But his 123 hits were the best by a rook since Ozzie Guillén in 1985.

CHAPTER 8:

PITCHER & CATCHER TIDBITS

QUIZ TIME!

1. Cuban pitcher Sandy Consuegra split time as a starter and in the bullpen. What was his best White Sox year when he went 16-3 with a 2.69 ERA, and made the All-Star team?

    a. 1950

    b. 1954

    c. 1957

    d. 1962

2. Backstopper Carlton "Pudge" Fisk spent 24 years in the majors. How many of those did he play on the South Side?

    a. 9

    b. 11

    c. 13

    d. 17

3. Who broke Bobby Thigpen's MLB record of 57 saves in 2008?

a. Brad Lidge

b. Jonathan Papelbon

c. Francisco Rodríguez

d. José Valverde

4. Wilson Álvarez was a regular White Sox starter in the `90s. In fact, he threw a no-no in only his second MLB start. Against whom?

a. Baltimore

b. Boston

c. Minnesota

d. Seattle

5. During the 1997 campaign, Álvarez was one of three White Sox traded to the Giants in the so-called "White Flag" deal. Which of the following was NOT one of the six S.F. players to come to Chicago?

a. Lorenzo Barceló

b. Mike Caruso

c. Brian Manning

d. Pat Rapp

6. Chicago catcher Ray Schalk dropped out of high school to focus on a technical trade. When advancement proved hard, he started to play pro ball. What was the trade he gave up?

a. Black and white photography

b. Linotype printing

c. Sheet metal worker

d. Stone cutting

7. Sherm Lollar was considered one of the best MLB catchers in the 1950s, earning seven trips to the All-Star Game. However, he was often overshadowed by which other catcher?

   a. Yogi Berra
   b. Clint Courtney
   c. Joe Garagiola
   d. Red Wilson

8. Ed Herrmann became known as one of the best knuckleball handlers in the AL. Which of the following knucklers was NOT one he handled with the Sox?

   a. Jim Bouton
   b. Eddie Fisher
   c. Hoyt Wilhelm
   d. Wilbur Wood

9. Billy Pierce was a slight but fiery lefty, and a principal player in Chicago's tremendous rivalry against the Yankees from the mid-1950s on. Which Yankee southpaw was his nemesis?

   a. Whitey Ford
   b. Lefty Gomez
   c. Ron Guidry
   d. Fritz Peterson

10. Bobby Jenks is third all-time in saves for Chicago, and once held the MLB record with 41 straight batters retired. How fast was his speediest pitch clocked?

a. 93 mph

b. 96 mph

c. 99 mph

d. 102 mph

11. Mark Buehrle tied Greg Maddux, Phil Niekro and Christy Mathewson with 200 innings in 14 straight seasons. What was the only Opening Day start he missed from 2002 to 2011?

a. 2004

b. 2006

c. 2007

d. 2009

12. Besides Chicago, Freddy García hurled for numerous other MLB teams, including the Mariners, Phillies, and Yankees. Which of the following countries is one he did NOT pitch in professionally?

a. China

b. Mexico

c. Taiwan

d. Venezuela

13. José Contreras pitched against an MLB team in Cuba in 1999, hurling eight shutout innings, fanning ten, and making scouts take notice. What was the visiting AL team?

a. Baltimore

b. Boston

c. Cleveland

d. Detroit

14. Tony Peña adopted a strange catching stance with no base runners, extending his left leg while squatting on his right. What was the reason for his unique stance?

    a. Because his left leg was slightly longer than his right
    b. Because that was the style in his native Dominican Republic
    c. To help his pitchers keep the ball low
    d. To relieve pressure on his injured left leg

15. A.J. Pierzynski caught for 18 years in the majors, including seven in Chicago. How many other catchers did he join in MLB history with more than 2,000 hits in his career?

    a. 7
    b. 8
    c. 12
    d. 14

16. One constant criticism of Pierzynski as a catcher was his habit of doing what to hitters, something he said isn't true.

    a. antagonizing
    b. chatting with
    c. insulting
    d. winding up

17. Though Pete Varney caught for the White Sox, he's perhaps more famous for his last-second two-point conversion catch allowing his college team to tie their archrivals. What was the game?

    a. Harvard-Yale
    b. Penn-Princeton

c. Ohio State-Michigan

d. Purdue-Illinois

18. "Sunday Teddy" Lyons spent his entire career with the White Sox, amassing 260 wins with a 3.67 ERA. What was his number retired by Chicago?

a. 8

b. 12

c. 16

d. 32

19. Ed Walsh managed to win a mere 40 games for Chicago in 1908. What was the all-time best career ERA he posted?

a. 1.68

b. 1.82

c. 1.99

d. 2.12

20. Jon Garland was drafted by the dreaded Cubs but ended up being traded in 1998 to the other Chicago team for another hurler having a down year. Who was he?

a. Jason Bere

b. Chad Bradford

c. Matt Karchner

d. Todd Rizzo

QUIZ ANSWERS

1. B - 1954

2. C - 13

3. C - Francisco Rodríguez

4. A - Baltimore

5. D - Pat Rapp

6. B - Linotype printing

7. A - Yogi Berra

8. A - Jim Bouton

9. A - Whitey Ford

10. D - 102 mph

11. C - 2007

12. C - Taiwan

13. A - Baltimore

14. C - To help his pitchers keep the ball low

15. B - 8

16. B - chatting with

17. A - Harvard-Yale (1968)

18. C - 16

19. B - 1.82

20. C - Matt Karchner

DID YOU KNOW?

1. Ray Schalk's small size allowed him to work behind the plate like a fifth infielder. In 1912, a policeman stopped Ray from entering the Comiskey Park locker room, mistaking him for a child.

2. LaMarr Hoyt was traded by the Yankees for shortstop Bucky Dent. He tied a Chicago record by winning his first nine decisions.

3. The ace of the Chicago staff in the '90s and the 1993 AL Cy Young winner, Jack McDowell set a modern mark by recording a decision in his first 27 starts.

4. Hoyt "Ol' Sarge" Wilhelm plied his knuckleball with a number of teams, but his best years were on the South Side. From 1963-1968, his ERA was at most 2.65, and he snagged 20+ saves in three seasons.

5. Keith Foulke was outstanding in Chicago's 1998 bullpen. He struggled a bit more in Boston, especially when he said he was more embarrassed to meet his teammates after rough outings than see "Johnny from Burger King" booing him.

6. When Carlton Fisk joined the White Sox in 1981, his favorite number 27 belonged to pitcher Ken Kravec. He switched things around, wearing 72 for the next 11 years in Chicago.

7. Both of Fisk's brothers, Calvin and Conrad, were drafted from their small New Hampshire town. Neither played in the majors: Calvin was inducted to fight in Vietnam, and Conrad hurt his arm.

8. After another injury in 1984, Fisk credited White Sox conditioning coach Phil Claussen for his physical recovery. Phil favored longer, more scientific weight-training sessions.

9. After throwing out 54% of runners in 1993, Ron Karkovice went on to manage the Gulf Coast Royals and the Camden River Sharks.

10. Catcher Sherm Lollar was selected for the Chicago White Sox All-Century Team on September 30, 2000.

CHAPTER 9:

ODDS & ENDS

QUIZ TIME!

1. The 1901 White Stockings depended on speed and scored a ton of runs. Which of the following players did NOT finish 1-2-3 in stolen bags that year?

   a. Clark Griffith

   b. Frank Isbell

   c. Fielder Jones

   d. Sam Mertes

2. What was the name of the league that changed its name to the American League in 1900?

   a. Midwestern

   b. National

   c. Nebraska State

   d. Western

3. During his long tenure as White Sox manager, Al López gained a nickname due to his Spanish ancestry and gentlemanly approach. What was it?

a. "El Español"

b. "El Matador"

c. "El Professor"

d. "El Señor"

4. When López's pro career as a ball player started in 1924, he was 16 and began to make about $150 per month. Where did he quit working to go pro?

a. Bakery

b. Bus terminal

c. Cigar factory

d. Orange juice factory

5. López decided to take advantage of Chicago's speed, and they proceeded to steal at least 100 bags a season from 1957 to 1961. Which of the following was NOT one of his speedsters?

a. Luis Aparicio

b. Nellie Fox

c. Bill Melton

d. Minnie Miñoso

6. Who was the first player to ever break the $10 million per year compensation mark? At the time (1995), he played for Cleveland, and later crushed the ball for Chicago.

a. Rubén Amaro, Jr.

b. Albert Belle

c. Manny Ramirez

d. Omar Vizquel

7. José Valentin bashed 136 homers while playing on the South Side from 2000 to 2004. Which Puerto Rican team did he buy after retiring?

    a. Arecibo Wolves

    b. Puerto Rico Islanders

    c. San Juan Senadores

    d. Santurce Crabbers

8. Ron Kittle was a key player on the 1983 "Winning Ugly" team that made the playoffs for the first time since taking the Series in 1959. How many games did the '83 version win?

    a. 89

    b. 95

    c. 99

    d. 101

9. Carlos Lee tied Jimmy Foxx and Ted Williams with 17 career grand slams, good for seventh spot on the all-time MLB list. What country was he from?

    a. Japan

    b. Nicaragua

    c. Panama

    d. Venezuela

10. Jermaine Dye was one of Chicago's heroes and the 2005 World Series MVP. Off which Astros reliever did he rip an RBI single, clinching the decisive Game 4 win?

    a. Roger Clemens

    b. Brad Lidge

c. Chad Qualls

d. Wandy Rodríguez

11. Three "clean" Sox from the 1919 group are now in the Hall of Fame. Which of the following is the odd man out?

a. Eddie Collins

b. Red Faber

c. Grover Loudermilk

d. Ray Schalk

12. Even though Charles Comiskey's reputation was sullied by the Black Sox Scandal, he was still enshrined as an executive in the Baseball hall of Fame. In what year?

a. 1934

b. 1939

c. 1946

d. 1956

13. Comiskey was notoriously "stingy", though his backers referred to him as "frugal". He even asked players to wash their own uniforms. Without free agency, players had to accept.

a. True

b. False

14. Before taking over in Chicago, Bill Veeck began the integration of the American League in Cleveland. Which African American did he first sign in 1947?

a. Willard Brown

b. Larry Doby

c. Hank Thompson

d. Jackie Robinson

15. Veeck started "innovating" in Milwaukee, holding weddings at home plate and scheduling morning games for nightshift workers. How much money did he have in his pocket upon arrival there?

a. $11

b. $55

c. $76

d. $157

16. What was Veeck's scheme dubbed when he took other teams' stars in their option years, leading to the valuable acquisitions of such players as Oscar Gamble and Richie Zisk?

a. Give Me Your Poor Options

b. Optical Option Illusions

c. Rent-A-Player

d. Veeck's Vouchers

17. Gary Peters was AL Rookie of the Year, winning 19 games on the Chicago mound in 1963. As well as being used as a pinch runner, he was a capable hitter. Against which team did he hit a grand slam in 1968?

a. Minnesota Twins

b. New York Yankees

c. Oakland A's

d. Washington Senators

18. Ed Walsh apparently threw a spitball that "disintegrated" on its way to the plate. He also struck out a batter in every inning of a single World Series game in 1906. Who was the only pitcher to ever do the same?

    a. Bob Gibson
    b. Denny McClain
    c. Jim Palmer
    d. Nolan Ryan

19. Johnny Mostil attempted suicide during spring training in 1927 but recovered to play again. Before that, in what category did he lead the AL during the 1926 season?

    a. Doubles
    b. Homers
    c. Runs
    d. Stolen bases

20. Edward "Cocky" Collins was an unusual commodity in the early 1900s, focused on both his baseball and education. What false name did he use as a minor leaguer to protect his collegiate status?

    a. Columbia
    b. Ruth
    c. Sheridan
    d. Sullivan

QUIZ ANSWERS

1. A - Clark Griffith

2. D - Western

3. D - "El Señor"

4. A - Bakery

5. C - Bill Melton

6. B - Albert Belle

7. D - Santurce Crabbers

8. C - 99

9. C - Panama

10. B - Brad Lidge

11. C - Grover Loudermilk

12. B - 1939

13. A - True

14. B - Larry Doby

15. A - $11

16. C - Rent-A-Player

17. B - New York Yankees

18. A - Bob Gibson

19. D - Stolen bases

20. D - Sullivan

DID YOU KNOW?

1. When Philly's Connie Mack sold Collins to Chicago in 1914 for $50,000, it was the highest ever paid for a player up to that point. Collins was exonerated in the Black Sox Scandal.

2. Southpaw is Chicago's mascot, representing a left-handed pitcher and the city's South Side. He was featured on a float during Barack Obama's inauguration.

3. In 2019, the revenue of the Chicago White Sox franchise amounted to $285 million.

4. Jerry Reinsdorf started his career as tax attorney with the IRS. He's been the head of the Bulls and White Sox for over 35 years.

5. In both sports, Reinsdorf has become known as an anti-union hardliner, as well as an advocate of the salary cap and revenue sharing, especially in basketball.

6. The name of Shoeless Joe Jackson's favorite bat was "Black Betsy", fashioned by a local fan (Charlie Ferguson) from the north side of a hickory tree and darkened with tobacco juice. The bat sold for $577,610 in 2001.

7. In 1922, Charlie Robertson became the first MLB player to ever throw a perfect game on the road—the fifth in history, in just his fourth start. His opponent that day, the Tigers, included Ty Cobb and Harry Heilmann and complained he

was messing with the ball, but AL President Ban Johnson let him off.

8. After (temporarily) retiring from basketball, Michael Jordan signed with the White Sox in 1994. Assigned to the Birmingham Barons, His Airness hit .202, made 11 outfield errors, and was nabbed stealing 18 times in 48 attempts. He returned to the Bulls for three more championships.

9. At the tender age of 75, Luke Appling jacked one over the left field fence in Washington's RFK Stadium in the 1982 Cracker Jack's Old-Timer's Classic.

10. Zeke Bonura played three years for the Sox but was already famous as the youngest ever athlete (at 16) to win an event at the 1925 National AAU Track and Field Championships, tossing the javelin 65.18 meters (213.10 feet).

CHAPTER 10:

WHO'S ON FIRST?

QUIZ TIME!

1. Frank Thomas is definitely the most prolific offensive player in White Sox history. Who's the only position player he ranks behind in terms of "Wins Above Replacement" (WAR)?

   a. Luke Appling
   b. Harold Baines
   c. Nellie Fox
   d. Jim Landis

2. When did "The Big Hurt" win his back-to-back AL MVP Awards?

   a. 1991-1992
   b. 1993-1994
   c. 1995-1996
   d. 1998-1999

3. Playing first for Chicago for 16 years, in how many offensive categories does Paul Konerko rank in the Top 4?

a. 5

b. 8

c. 12

d. 15

4. After Konerko caught the last out in the 2005 Series sweep over Houston, who did he present the ball to?

a. Chairman Jerry Reinsdorf

b. His daughter Amelia

c. His mother Elena

d. His wife Jennifer Wells

5. In 2013, José Abreu defected from Cuba and established residency in the Dominican Republic to test free agent waters. How much was first his 6-year contract with Chicago worth?

a. $24 million

b. $46 million

c. $68 million

d. $80 million

6. What did Abreu claim he ate on the flight from Haiti to the U.S. after he was smuggled into the former country from Cuba?

a. Haitian delicacies

b. Ropa Vieja (Cuban-style shredded beef)

c. The pages of his fake Haitian passport

d. Typical airline food

7. Dick Allen had a big impact in Chicago despite his short time on the South Side. In what minor league city did Allen suffer racial harassment as his career kick-started?

    a. Clearwater, Florida
    b. Little Rock, Arkansas
    c. Reading, Pennsylvania
    d. Williamsport, Pennsylvania

8. When Allen's dinger cleared the Connie Mack Stadium roof, which opponent said, "Now I know why the (Phillies) fans boo Richie all the time. When he hits a home run, there's no souvenir."?

    a. George Foster
    b. Jim Rice
    c. Reggie Smith
    d. Willie Stargell

9. In 1943, Zeke Bonura was responsible for organizing baseball championships in the Algerian desert in WWII. Who won the final three-game series there?

    a. Algerian Streetwalkers
    b. Casablanca Yankees
    c. Marrakesh Mountain Men
    d. Tangier Tigers

10. When Bonura hit a career-high .345 in 1937, which of the following brilliant batters did he NOT finish behind?

    a. Joe DiMaggio
    b. Lou Gehrig

c. Charlie Gehringer

d. Pinky Whitney

11. Greg Walker may be best known for his contribution as the White Sox 2005 hitting coach. He played eight years for the White Sox, except for the last _____ of his career.

   a. 14 days

   b. 14 games

   c. 3 months

   d. 30 minutes

12. With Oakland in 2006, almost 10 years past his Chicago prime, Frank Thomas blasted 39 homers. How old was he at the time?

   a. 34

   b. 36

   c. 38

   d. 41

13. Jerry Reinsdorf lauded Thomas, saying: "When your career comes to an end and your body of work is compared to Hall of Famers like Mel Ott, Babe Ruth, and Ted Williams, you truly rank among baseball _____."

   a. figureheads

   b. gods

   c. kings

   d. royalty

14. What was the name of the Chicago first baseman who was reputedly the brainchild behind the Black Sox conspiracy?

a. Arnold "Chick" Gandil

b. Dickey Kerr

c. Fred McMullin

d. William "Sleepy Bill" Burns

15. Who was the first baseman on the "Hitless Wonders" White Sox squad that snatched the 1906 Series away from the championed Cubs?

a. Jiggs Donahue

b. Eddie Hahn

c. Billy Sullivan

d. Lee Tannehill

16. Despite his relatively anemic bat (granted it was the dead-ball era), Jiggs Donahue set the record for putouts by a first baseman in 1907, a mark which still stands. How many did he grab?

a. 1,688

b. 1,767

c. 1,846

d. 1,957

17. When Ted Kluszewski was traded from Cincinnati to Chicago, he didn't commit a single error in 31 games, batted .297, and helped the "Go-Go" Sox clinch the AL pennant and win the '59 World Series.

a. True

b. False

18. Due to wartime travel restrictions from 1943 to 1945, the Reds held spring training in the Midwest. Groundskeeper Matty Schwab saw Kluszewski, then a college student, hitting balls where no Red could reach. What was the university?

    a. Cincinnati
    b. Indiana
    c. Illinois
    d. Xavier

19. Greg Walker played first for the "Winning Ugly" Sox of 1983. Which opposing coach was responsible for creating the rallying cry, saying the Sox weren't playing well, just "winning ugly"?

    a. Pat Corrales / Indians
    b. Ralph Houk / Red Sox
    c. Dick Howser / Royals
    d. Doug Rader / Rangers

20. Jim Thome was dealt by Cleveland to Chicago prior to the 2006 season. What award did he win after his arrival in the Windy City?

    a. AL Comeback Player of the Year
    b. AL MVP
    c. Historic Achievement Award
    d. Silver Slugger

QUIZ ANSWERS

1. A - Luke Appling

2. B - 1993-1994

3. C - 12 categories

4. A - Chairman Jerry Reinsdorf

5. C - $68 million

6. C - The first page of his fake Cuban passport

7. B - Little Rock, Arkansas

8. D - Willie Stargell

9. B - Casablanca Yankees (consisting of medics)

10. D - Pinky Whitney

11. B - 14 games

12. C - 38

13. D - royalty

14. A - Arnold "Chick" Gandil

15. A - Jiggs Donahue

16. C - 1,846

17. B - False / He was traded from Pittsburgh.

18. B - Indiana

19. D - Doug Rader / Rangers

20. A - AL Comeback Player of the Year

DID YOU KNOW?

1. Unfortunately, Frank Thomas, who had waited 16 years to get to the World Series with the Sox, was injured in 2005 and unable to participate.

2. Jim Thome was active in philanthropy throughout his career and earned two Marvin Miller Man of the Year Awards as well as a Lou Gehrig Memorial Award for community involvement.

3. In November 2014, the White Sox reported a two-year, $25 million deal with first baseman Adam LaRoche. In March 2016, Adam said he would "step away from baseball", leaving another $13 million on the table.

4. It turned out the reason for LaRoche's sudden retirement was the White Sox had restricted his 14-year-old son from entering the clubhouse every day. Chicago exec Kenny Williams defended the decision: "Name one job in the country where you can bring your child to work every day."

5. Carlos Lee maintained a .988 fielding percentage at first and in left over a 14-year career. He has a fan club called "Los Caballitos" or "The Little Horses", maybe from the cattle ranches he runs.

6. Kevin Youkilis was traded by the Red Sox to the White Sox in June 2012. He was quickly named AL Player of the Week,

and manager Ventura noted his "grinder mentality" and how he fit in well with Chicago teammates.

7. Justin Morneau played the 2016 season in Chicago. According to his Portland Winter Hawks hockey coach, Mike Williamson: "We told him he should go to hockey because not many Canadian guys end up going very far in baseball. He showed us otherwise."

8. Adam Dunn is tied for the most Opening Day homers in MLB history with eight. He's also knotted with Bo Jackson for fifth most "Golden Sombreros" (four strikeouts in one game) with 19.

9. John Kruk came to Chicago in 1995 principally as a Designated Hitter. He retired after a season due to chronic knee soreness, and released a book, "I Ain't an Athlete, Lady".

10. Nick Swisher was traded by the A's to Chicago as part of the former team's rebuilding effort. He batted a measly .219 on the South Side, but became a fan favorite, nonetheless.

CHAPTER 11:

WHO'S GOT SECOND?

QUIZ TIME!

1. Eddie Collins became only the sixth player in MLB history to join the 3,000-hit club, and he did it with the lowest number of homers of any on the list. How many did he squeak over the fences?

    a. 39

    b. 47

    c. 56

    d. 70

2. In 1910, Collins settled at second base, became the first AL player to ever steal more than 80 bases in a season, and played on the first of his six World Series championship teams.

    a. True

    b. False

3. Nellie Fox showed baseball promise at an early age growing up in rural PA. Who wrote a letter to Philly's Connie Mack requesting a trial for the 16-year-old Fox?

a. His father

b. His mother

c. His pastor

d. His teacher

4. After Fox was traded by the Philadelphia A's to Chicago in 1949, he stayed for 14 seasons and made 12 All-Star appearances. Who was he traded for?

a. Al Gettel

b. Ernest Groth

c. Orval Grove

d. Joe Tipton

5. Ray Durham put up big Chicago numbers at second from 2000 on. Which of the following is NOT on the elite player list he joined with at least 15 homers, 100 runs, 20 steals, a .450 slugging percentage and 65 RBIs in three straight seasons?

a. Hank Aaron

b. Willie Mays

c. Joe Morgan

d. Ryne Sandberg

6. Durham left the White Sox as the all-time best in leadoff homers. How many did he clock?

a. 12

b. 16

c. 20

d. 25

7. Tadahito Iguchi was an integral piece to the 2005 championship puzzle in Chicago. In what position in the lineup did he normally bat?

    a. Leadoff
    b. Second
    c. Seventh
    d. Eighth

8. In Game 2 of the '05 ALDS, Iguchi went deep against the Red Sox to turn the contest the White Sox's way. Who was the unlucky Boston pitcher?

    a. Bronson Arroyo
    b. Jonathan Papelbon
    c. Tim Wakefield
    d. David Wells

9. Who covered second on the 1977 "South Side Hitmen"?

    a. Alex Bannister
    b. Clay Carroll
    c. Chet Lemon
    d. Jorge Orta

10. Gordon Beckham turned into a top-notch second baseman. In what position did he start out as a rookie in 2009?

    a. Center field
    b. Left field
    c. Shortstop
    d. Third base

11. Joey Cora had a bit of a hot bat in Chicago's 1993 AL West title run. What were the numbers of doubles and triples he smacked?

    a. 12/10
    b. 15/13
    c. 18/17
    d. 22/16

12. When Alexei Ramírez bashed his fourth grand slam in 2008, he broke the rookie record and guaranteed a playoff against the Twins for the AL Central title. Who was the sad Tigers pitcher who gave up the blast?

    a. Gary Glover
    b. Zach Miner
    c. Fernando Rodney
    d. Dontrelle Willis

13. Julio Franco's bid in 1994 to reach 100 RBIs with Chicago was cut short by the MLB strike. Which Japanese team did he then help to its best season ever?

    a. Chiba Lotte Marines
    b. Hanshin Tigers
    c. Hiroshima Carp
    d. Yakult Swallows

14. After his playing career, Omar Vizquel managed Chicago's Class-A Advanced team, the Winston-Salem Dash. Which AA affiliate was he promoted to manage in 2017?

a. Birmingham Barons
b. Charlotte Knights
c. Great Falls Voyagers
d. Kannapolis Cannon Ballers

15. Chris Getz led the AL in stolen base percentage (92.6%) in 2009. How many multi-hit games did he have that year to tie for first among rookies?

    a. 20
    b. 24
    c. 28
    d. 37

16. Orlando Hudson lamented the apparent racism active in free agency in 2010: "Guy with 27 home runs and 81 RBIs and can't get a job." Which African American did he refer to?

    a. Adrian Beltre
    b. Jermaine Dye
    c. Vladimir Guerrero
    d. Gary Sheffield

17. April 11, 2011, saw Brent Lillibridge smack a fifth-inning homer off Dallas Braden. What was the historic number of that dinger in 112 years of White Sox history?

    a. 5,000th
    b. 7,000th
    c. 10,000th
    d. 13,000th

18. While playing in the Cardinals organization, which attribute was Tyler Greene lauded for every year from 2006 to 2009?

    a. Best Base Runner
    b. Best Chance to Succeed
    c. Best Infield Arm
    d. Best-Looking Player

19. Mark Teahen was featured in the book and movie "Moneyball" as the player who had the potential to become the next _____. Who was the target?

    a. José Canseco
    b. Jason Giambi
    c. Brett Lawrie
    d. Mark McGwire

20. Before becoming manager of the infamous 1919 White Sox team, Kid Gleason played second for a number of clubs. Which was his first in 1888?

    a. Baltimore Orioles
    b. Philadelphia A's
    c. Philadelphia Quakers
    d. New York Giants

QUIZ ANSWERS

1. B - 47

2. A - True

3. B - His mother

4. D - Joe Tipton

5. D - Ryne Sandberg

6. C - 20

7. B - Second

8. D - David Wells

9. D - Jorge Orta

10. D - Third base

11. B - 15/13

12. A - Gary Glover

13. A - Chiba Lotte Marines

14. A - Birmingham Barons

15. C - 28

16. B - Jermaine Dye

17. C - 10,000[th]

18. C - Best Infield Arm

19. B - Jason Giambi

20. C - Philadelphia Quakers

DID YOU KNOW?

1. Kid Gleason had two plate appearances in one 1912 game, placing him in an elite group of 29 men to play pro ball in four decades.

2. Willie Harris pinch hit successfully in Game 4 of the 2005 Series against Houston. He then scored on Jermaine Dye's single—the only run of the decisive contest.

3. In 1996, Tony Phillips drew 125 walks on the South Side, leading the league, and parlayed some into 119 runs on the season.

4. Besides Boston and Oakland, Mike Andrews spent a couple of years playing in Chicago. He also served more than 25 years as the chairman of The Jimmy Fund, raising money to fight cancer.

5. Scott Fletcher became the first pro athlete in the Dallas/Fort Worth area to make more than a million a year. A certain owner of the Rangers, George W. Bush, named his dog after Fletcher.

6. In September 2004, Julio Cruz was inducted into the Hispanic Heritage Hall of Fame in a Seattle ceremony.

7. Frank "Bald Eagle" Isbell was one of only two White Sox hitters to bat above .260, but Chicago won the 1906 Series anyway.

8. Strong-armed Venezuelan Fred Manrique was the youngest player in the majors when he broke in at 19 with Toronto.

9. With the White Sox in 1942, Don Kolloway led the AL in doubles (40), and was among the leaders in stolen bags (16) and times caught stealing (14).

10. 2019 White Sox hitting coach Frank Menechino was one of the players who dared to cross the picket lines in 1995 as a replacement player. He was thus ineligible for the MLB Players Association.

CHAPTER 12:

WHO'S AT THE HOT CORNER?

QUIZ TIME!

1. When Robin Ventura was hired by the White Sox to manage the team in 2011, how many former Chicago players did he join who had later become Sox managers?

    a. 9
    b. 12
    c. 16
    d. 21

2. Ventura was beaned by a Texas Rangers pitcher in 1993, and a bench-clearing brawl ensued (which was later named the top dustup ever by ESPN's SportsCenter). Who was on the mound?

    a. Jeff Bronkey
    b. Hector Fajardo
    c. Nolan Ryan
    d. Mike Schooler

3. Soon after helping the Sox win the 2005 Series, Joe Crede was honored by his hometown and granted the key to the city. Where's this fine community located?

    a. Bowie, Maryland
    b. Fatima, Missouri
    c. Westphalia, Missouri
    d. Bozeman, Montana

4. "Beltin'" Bill Melton made steady progress through the Sox system, always showing the two traits he became known for in his career: a powerful bat and what type of fielding?

    a. bad
    b. fluid
    c. outstanding
    d. questionable

5. Melton became a mainstay at third for the Sox, but his production declined in 1972 when he missed most of the season after trying to cushion his son's fall from the garage roof.

    a. True
    b. False

6. In 1964, Pete Ward was able to avoid his "sophomore jinx". How many runs did he drive in that year?

    a. 76
    b. 82
    c. 94
    d. 111

7. Willie Kamm was the first MLB player to be signed straight from the minors for $100,000 in 1923. What special play was he a master of?

   a. Drag bunt
   b. Hidden ball trick
   c. Hook slide
   d. Suicide squeeze

8. Chicago gambled on Eric Soderholm's dodgy knee, and it paid off as he helped the South Side Hitmen almost win the West in 1977. How many dingers did he have after the All-Star break?

   a. 25
   b. 20
   c. 16
   d. 13

9. After his retirement in 1982, Soderholm became a scout, started youth baseball camps, and turned into a private hitting instructor. What did the center called Soderworld that he opened offer?

   a. Batting machines
   b. Healing arts
   c. Natural foods
   d. Youth counseling

10. Buck Weaver switched from short to third in 1917 due to the arrival of another ace. Who was he?

    a. Shoeless Joe Jackson
    b. Bird Lynn

c. Swede Risberg

d. Pants Rowland

11. Even though many reporters suspected a Chicago fix in 1919, Weaver's stellar play was commended. "Buck is Chicago's one big _____ ; long may he fight and smile," one wrote.

a. batter

b. gentleman

c. hero

d. Sock

12. In what year did George Kell win his only batting title (.343), defying Ted "The Splendid Splinter" Williams his third Triple Crown?

a. 1943

b. 1947

c. 1949

d. 1951

13. Kell later became a Tigers broadcaster with his inimitable Arkansan accent. Which slugger once broke Kell's jaw while Kell played third base and still made the play?

a. Joe DiMaggio

b. Hank Greenberg

c. Connie Mack

d. Johnny Mize

14. Dick Allen came to the Sox as a third baseman but was switched to first and thus could concentrate more on

hitting. Which "low-key" manager engineered this 1972 change?

  a. Don Gutteridge
  b. Les Moss
  c. Eddy Stanky
  d. Chuck Tanner

15. Allen became the first batter in baseball's "modern era" to hit two inside-the-park homers in the same game. Who was the hapless opposing pitcher who yielded both?

  a. Bert Blyleven
  b. Gaylord Perry
  c. Luis Tiant
  d. Eddie Watt

16. In 2016, Todd Frazier finished second to Giancarlo Stanton in the MLB Home Run Derby. How many homers did Todd hit in total, compared to Stanton's 61?

  a. 35
  b. 42
  c. 55
  d. 60

17. Gordon Beckham was the second position player in his 2008 draft class to make his debut when he played at third in Chicago after 364 days in the minors. Who was the first?

  a. Conor Gillaspie / Giants
  b. Buster Posey / Giants
  c. Kyle Skipworth / Marlins
  d. Justin Smoak / Giants

18. Juan Uribe was always more comfortable on the South Side, batting .315, than on the road. What was his batting average in unfriendly confines in 2004?

    a. .208
    b. .228
    c. .248
    d. .269

19. Brett Lawrie was drafted as the 16th overall pick by the Brewers in 2008 and became the fourth-highest Canadian to reach the bigs. Which of the following Canucks was NOT drafted higher?

    a. Philippe Aumont
    b. Owen Caissie
    c. Jeff Francis
    d. Adam Loewen

20. Conor Gillaspie led the Cape Cod Baseball League in hitting (.345) in 2007, taking his squad to the championship series, only to miss the finals due to school. What was his team?

    a. Brewster Whitecaps
    b. Chatham Anglers
    c. Falmouth Commodores
    d. Wareham Gatemen

QUIZ ANSWERS

1. C - 16

2. C - Nolan Ryan

3. C - Westphalia, MO

4. D - questionable

5. A - True

6. C - 94

7. B - Hidden ball trick

8. C - 16

9. B - Healing arts

10. C - Swede Risberg

11. C - hero

12. C - 1949

13. A - Joe DiMaggio

14. D - Chuck Tanner

15. A - Bert Blyleven

16. B - 42

17. A - Conor Gillaspie

18. C - .248

19. B - Owen Caissie

20. C - Falmouth Commodores

DID YOU KNOW?

1. Dick Allen's batting accomplishments with the Sox, especially in his '72 MVP season, are claimed to have saved the franchise, rumored to have been on the verge of a move to Seattle.

2. Josh Fields became the third White Sox to belt a homer in his first major league at-bat in 2006, following Carlos Lee (1999) and Miguel Olivo (2002).

3. Mark Teahen came to Chicago in a trade with Kansas City. He was awarded the 2009 Hutch Award given to the player who "best exemplifies the fighting spirit and competitive desire" of Fred Hutchinson.

4. Wilson Betemit was signed by the Braves out of the Dominican Republic at 14 years old. Since MLB teams can't sign players younger than 16, Atlanta forked over a $100,000 fine.

5. When Al Smith was traded to the Sox by Cleveland, he replaced the popular Minnie Miñoso. When Al slumped, Bill Veeck declared an "Al Smith Night" allowing anyone named Smith(e), Smythe or Schmidt in free.

6. Sadly, Tim Hulett's 6-year-old son was hit and killed by a car in 1992. This led to the adoption by the MLB of two Family Leave lists: one for bereavement and one for paternity leave.

7. Despite being only a utility infielder in 1919, Fred McMullin overheard conversations about the Black Sox conspiracy, and threatened to report the other players if he wasn't included.

8. McMullin served as Chicago's "advance scout" for the Series on their Cincinnati foe, and may have delivered a false report to the "clean Sox" on the Reds' pitching defects.

9. Lee Tannehill, brother of pitcher Jesse, was the first player to ever homer in Comiskey Park in 1910.

10. Buck Weaver successfully sued Chicago owner Charles Comiskey for his 1921 salary. He tried to be reinstated to baseball no fewer than six times before dying of a heart attack in 1956 at 65.

CHAPTER 13:

WHO'S AT SHORT?

QUIZ TIME!

1. What minor league team did Luke Appling briefly appear for before spending 20 years with the White Sox?

    a. Atlanta Crackers

    b. Asheville Tourists

    c. Carolina Mudcats

    d. Greensboro Grasshoppers

2. In high school, Appling was left-handed like his father. But he forced himself to play right-handed because he desperately wanted to be a shortstop.

    a. True

    b. False

3. When Luis "Little Louie" Aparicio was AL MVP runner-up and helped the "Go-Go" Sox win the AL championship in 1959, in which of the following categories did he NOT lead the league?

a. Assists by Shortstop

b. Batting Average

c. Putouts by Shortstop

d. Stolen bases

4. Which famous slugging contemporary of Aparicio's called him "the best shortstop he had ever seen"?

   a. Ernie Banks

   b. Yogi Berra

   c. Mickey Mantle

   d. Ted Williams

5. What nickname did Alexei Ramírez earn from manager Ozzie Guillén for his combination of height, power, speed, and strong throwing arm?

   a. The Caribbean Killer

   b. The Caribbean Rocket

   c. The Cuban Conundrum

   d. The Cuban Missile

6. When Ramírez clubbed his fourth grand slam as a 2008 rookie, whose MLB record did he break?

   a. Aaron Judge / Yankees

   b. Willie McCovey / Giants

   c. Shane Spencer / Yankees

   d. Dizzy Trout / Tigers

7. How many years did Ozzie Guillén spend with the White Sox, first as a shortstop and then a manager?

   a. 17

   b. 20

c. 21

d. 25

8. In 1992, Guillén crashed into another Chicago outfielder, seriously injuring his knee, reducing his effectiveness at short and on the base paths for the rest of his career. Who was the culprit?

a. Daryl Boston

b. Lance Johnson

c. Sammy Sosa

d. Tim Raines

9. After receiving a signing bonus of $2,164,000 from the White Sox in 2013, which Chicago affiliate was Tim Anderson assigned to play with?

a. Bristol White Sox

b. Hickory Crawdads

c. Kannapolis Intimidators

d. Winston-Salem Dash

10. Despite a career-high 167 hits in 2019, Anderson had the lowest fielding percentage of all MLB shortstops with at least 84 appearances. What was his success (or lack thereof) rate?

a. .962

b. .951

c. .945

d. .933

11. Which Chicago shortstop was moved around the infield in 2008 to make way for the up and coming Orlando Cabrera?

    a. Alexei Ramírez
    b. Joe Crede
    c. Juan Uribe
    d. Pablo Ozuna

12. Omar Vizquel won 11 Gold Gloves at short during his exemplary career. Who did he tie for most consecutive games at short without an error (since surpassed)?

    a. Rick Burleson
    b. Cal Ripken, Jr.
    c. Ozzie Smith
    d. Honus Wagner

13. Besides the White Sox, how many other pro outfits (including in Japan and South Korea) did Júlio Franco suit up for in his career?

    a. 7
    b. 9
    c. 11
    d. 13

14. Who did Jimmy Rollins compete with for the shortstop spot in Chicago in 2016?

    a. Tim Anderson
    b. Matt Davids
    c. Mike Olt
    d. Tyler Saladino

15. After undergoing Tommy John surgery, how many White Sox games did Tyler Saladino appear in during the 2016 / 2017 seasons?

    a. 154

    b. 172

    c. 196

    d. 222

16. Gordon Beckham cracked his first big-league homer on June 20, 2009, in the "MLB Civil Rights Game". Who was the curve-hanging Reds pitcher?

    a. Homer Bailey

    b. Jared Burton

    c. Johnny Cueto

    d. Matt Maloney

17. When Brent Lillibridge was traded by Atlanta to Chicago in 2008, who did the Sox give up besides Javier Vázquez?

    a. Gregor Blanco

    b. Tyler Flowers

    c. Jon Gilmore

    d. Boone Logan

18. Buck Weaver "who guarded third like his life" also played short for Chicago. Who said he was an inspiration to all around him because of his optimism and dedication to restoring his name?

    a. His mother, Susan

    b. His niece, Patricia Anderson

c. His teammate, Swede Risberg

d. Phillies manager, Charley Dooin

19. Lee "BeeBee" Richard played short for Chicago, but his defense was poor. Which team was he swapped to?

a. Brewers

b. Cardinals

c. Cubs

d. Twins

20. Appearing for the Sox in 1999, Jason Dellaero still ranks high in numerous offensive categories at his alma mater. What was the university?

a. Florida Institute of Technology

b. Florida State

c. North Florida

d. South Florida

QUIZ ANSWERS

1. A - Atlanta Crackers

2. A - True

3. B - Batting Average

4. D - Ted Williams

5. D - The Cuban Missile

6. C - Shane Spencer / Yankees

7. C - 21

8. D - Tim Raines

9. C - Kannapolis Intimidators (NC)

10. B - .951

11. C - Juan Uribe

12. B - Cal Ripken, Jr.

13. B - 9

14. D - Tyler Saladino

15. B - 172

16. C - Johnny Cueto

17. D - Boone Logan

18. B - His niece, Patricia Anderson

19. B - Cardinals

20. D - South Florida

DID YOU KNOW?

1. Ángel Sánchez made a quick Chicago tour, playing in a single game. Hitless in two at-bats, he went on the disabled list, dropped down to the Charlotte Knights, and finally released.

2. Baseball historian Bill James claimed Scott Fletcher "didn't do anything exceptionally well" and basically "filled a slot". He then ranked Scott as the 85th best all-time shortstop.

3. Mike Caruso was brought up in 1999 to be the Sox's starting shortstop. His Chicago stint lasted only two years after which he played for the Royals, South Georgia Peanuts, and Joliet JackHammers.

4. Jerry Dybzinski started 82 games at short for the 1983 Sox. Alas, he made a baserunning mistake in the ALCS against Baltimore, overrunning second while third was occupied by Vance Law.

5. Swede Risberg's dismal slump at the end of the 1917 season only allowed him two pinch-hit appearances in the 1917 Series win over the New York Giants.

6. Risberg was highly praised by the Atlanta Constitution before the 1919 Series. He was "a miracle man" who had "blossomed out as a wonder" making phenomenal plays at short.

7. Ron Hansen was traded by the Orioles to Chicago along with Hoyt Wilhelm for Luis Aparacio in late 1962. He led

AL shortstops three times in double plays and four times in assists.

8. Leury García made Chicago's 2014 Opening Day roster with Gordon Beckham and Jeff Keppinger both hurt. He led the AL with 11 sacrifice hits in 2019.

9. Along with Luke Appling, Red Faber and Orval Grove, Lee Tannehill played his entire career on the South Side.

10. Al Weis only managed seven career regular-season homers, but his blast in Game 5 of the 1969 Series helped the Miracle Mets to an improbable victory.

CHAPTER 14:

THE OUTFIELD GANG

QUIZ TIME!

1. Besides numerous outstanding seasons in Chicago's outfield, which of the following positions did Harold Baines NOT hold with the Sox?

    a. Coach
    b. Culture officer
    c. Spring training instructor
    d. Team ambassador

2. Baines is tied for seventh all time in MLB walk-off homers. How many did he send into the skies?

    a. 5
    b. 7
    c. 10
    d. 13

3. Johnny Mostil patrolled the Sox outfield in 1918 and again from 1921 to 1929. What was the record number of runs he scored in the '25 season?

a. 125

b. 135

c. 150

d. 160

4. In the '60s, Mostil coached at the Chicago White Sox Boys Camp. Where's this sports facility located?

   a. Bosstown, Wisconsin

   b. Brothertown, Wisconsin

   c. Random Lake, Wisconsin

   d. Sheboygan, Wisconsin

5. What word was used to describe the outfield grab made by Jim Landis to rob the Dodgers' Jim Gilliam in Game 5 of the 1959 Series?

   a. average

   b. iconic

   c. impossible

   d. unlikely

6. How many consecutive times did Landis haul in an AL Gold Glove Award while with the Sox?

   a. 4

   b. 5

   c. 7

   d. 8

7. Two of Chet Lemon's three All-Star appearances occurred with Chicago in 1978 and 1979. With whom did he win the Series in 1984?

a. Detroit Tigers

b. Los Angeles Dodgers

c. New York Yankees

d. Oakland A's

8. An integral part of the South Side Hitmen in '77, Chet Lemon had an OPS of .803 that year. What does that acronym stand for??

a. On-Base Plus Slugging

b. On-Base Plus Swinging

c. On-Point Plus Steals

d. Over-Production Stat

9. In what offensive category did Lance Johnson lead the AL from 1991 to 1994?

a. Doubles

b. Singles

c. Steals

d. Triples

10. In which category was Lance Johnson the only player to lead both the AL and NL, doing so in back-to-back seasons in 1995 and 1996 with the White Sox and Mets?

a. Bunts

b. Hits

c. Putouts

d. Sacrifice flies

11. One Chicago GM uses the example of outfielder Aaron Rowand as a player who arrived in the bigs but had to

return to the minors for necessary seasoning. Who was the exec?

a. Eddie Einhorn
b. Rick Hahn
c. Roland Hemond
d. Ron Schueler

12. Finally, at the end of 2005, Rowand's outstanding outfield play turned him into trade bait. For whom?

a. Bobby Jenks
b. Michael Morse
c. Jim Thome
d. Ryan Sweeney

13. Who did Fielder Jones begin his pro career with in 1896?

a. Brooklyn Bridegrooms
b. Brooklyn Superbas
c. Louisville Colonels
d. Washington Senators

14. After winning the 1906 Series with Chicago, Jones also managed the Sox. He later tried his hand in the newly formed Federal League with less success. With which team?

a. Baltimore Terrapins
b. Chicago Whales
c. Newark Peppers
d. St. Louis Terriers

15. Happy Felsch was one of the best AL hitters from 1916 to 1920. How did onlookers know that he was in on the Black Sox Scandal?

    a. He arrives at the first game with two left shoes.
    b. He misplayed flyballs in critical situations.
    c. He stumbled often on the base paths.
    d. He was hit in the head by a flyball.

16. In what year did centerfielder Tommie Agee win the Rookie of the Year with the White Sox?

    a. 1960
    b. 1963
    c. 1966
    d. 1969

17. In 1983, Rudy Law set the White Sox record for stolen bases in a single season. How many did he nab?

    a. 57
    b. 67
    c. 77
    d. 85

18. Law blasted the ball to all corners in the '83 ALCS against the Orioles, batting .389, but his teammates didn't join in. How many runs did Chicago manage while losing the series, 3-1?

    a. 3
    b. 5
    c. 7
    d. 8

19. Ken Griffey, Jr. squeezed in only 41 Sox games, but his deadeye throws in the 2008 AL Central tiebreaker win over the Twins assured victory. Who was the sorry Minnesota base runner?

    a. Boof Bonser
    b. Michael Cuddyer
    c. Nick Punto
    d. Denard Span

20. Minnie Miñoso was the first Black Cuban to grace MLB in 1948 and the first Black to ever play with the White Sox. What was the first of his five names upon birth?

    a. Adonis
    b. Calixto
    c. Saturnino
    d. Yoelvis

QUIZ ANSWERS

1. B - Culture officer

2. C - 10

3. B - 135

4. B - Brothertown, WI

5. B - iconic

6. B - 5

7. A - Detroit Tigers

8. A - On-Base Plus Slugging

9. D - Triples

10. B - Hits

11. B - Rick Hahn

12. C - Jim Thome

13. A - Brooklyn Bridegrooms

14. D - St. Louis Terriers

15. B - He misplayed flyballs in critical situations.

16. C - 1966

17. C - 77

18. A - 3

19. B - Michael Cuddyer

20. C - Saturnino

DID YOU KNOW?

1. Minnie Miñoso was pretty good at getting on base, leading the AL in times hit by pitch 10 times, and holding the career mark from 1959 to 1985.

2. Babe Ruth claimed that he modeled his hitting technique after the sublime Shoeless Joe Jackson.

3. Despite his sizzling bat in the 1919 Series, Shoeless Joe Jackson appeared to allow an unusually high number of Cincinnati triples to bounce around in his left-field territory.

4. Paul Konerko once admitted that outfielder Magglio Ordóñez was the best all-around player he had ever lined up next to in his career.

5. After success with both the Tigers and Sox, Magglio announced he'd run for office in his native Venezuela, and was soon elected mayor of a municipality there in 2013.

6. Jermaine Dye's production in 2006 even surpassed his stellar 2005 Series year. In '06, he won a Silver Slugger Award and the right to hang out at the All-Star Game.

7. In 1962, Floyd Robinson made MLB history with six singles in six at-bats. He the 18th player in AL history to go 6-for-6 in a game and sixth to do it with all singles.

8. Puerto Rican Alex Ríos won the Fielding Bible Award for right fielders in 2007. Rather than a religious award, the honor trumpets the best defensive players in each position.

9. Avisaíl García is heralded for his resemblance in appearance and with the bat to his former Tigers teammate Miguel Cabrera, netting him the nickname "Mini Miggy".

10. Taft "Taffy" Wright played almost his entire career in Chicago, racking up 100+ hits every year on the South Side and a batting average over .300 four times. He was originally traded for none other than Gee Walker.

CHAPTER 15:

THE HEATED RIVALRIES

QUIZ TIME!

1. One White Sox closer quipped, "Unless they (the Twins) have some deal with the devil up there, I don't see it happening again." Who was referring to Minnesota's lucky 2003 season?

   a. Bartolo Colón
   b. Gary Glover
   c. Billy Koch
   d. Damaso Marte

2. According to knowrivalry.com, the White Sox's biggest rivals are the crosstown Cubs with 38.46 "rival points". Who's second with 28.58?

   a. Cleveland
   b. Detroit
   c. Kansas City
   d. Minnesota

3. Which is the only team that has shared the same division as the White Sox since 1901?

   a. Indians
   b. Royals
   c. Tigers
   d. Twins

4. What was the name given to the one-game tiebreaker in 2008 to determine the ultimate winner of the AL Central Division between the White Sox and Twins?

   a. The Blackout Game
   b. The Blowout Game
   c. The Greatest Rivals Game
   d. MLB Slugfest

5. Just prior to the aforementioned tiebreaker, the White Sox had to make up (and win) a game rained out earlier to force the final showdown against the Twins. Who was the make-up foe?

   a. Boston
   b. Cleveland
   c. Detroit
   d. Seattle

6. What is the all-time series tally between the two great Chicago baseball teams, the White Sox and Cubs?

   a. 59-59
   b. 65-63
   c. 69-53
   d. 72-46

7. The Twins and the Sox have an equal number of AL pennants (6) and World Series triumphs (3).

    a. True
    b. False

8. Chicago's "good" rivalries with Detroit teams extends to other pro sports. What edges do the Tigers have over the Sox in World Series wins and AL Central division titles respectively?

    a. 2-1 / 2-1
    b. 3-2 / 3-2
    c. 4-3 / 4-3
    d. 5-4 / 6-5

9. When the Royals started 2018 terribly, Tim Anderson's blast (and subsequent chirping) cleared both Kansas City's and Chicago's benches. What did KC manager Ned Yost call the near bust-up?

    a. A bad moon rising
    b. A drop in the bucket
    c. A sign of things to come
    d. A tea party

10. The White Sox and Yankees competed hard for pennants in the 1950s and '60s when New York was the biggest American city in population, and Chicago second. When did the rivalry start?

    a. 1901
    b. 1913

c. 1932

d. 1946

11. Chicago fans claim they were the Sox before Boston was. In what year did Chicago steal Boston's thunder by preventing a Series repeat for the latter?

    a. 1906

    b. 1919

    c. 1959

    d. 2005

12. The fact that Milwaukee is geographically so close to Chicago makes the two cities natural rivals. Who killed this possibility by moving the Brewers to the NL in 1998?

    a. Bowie Kuhn

    b. Bud Selig

    c. Fay Vincent

    d. Peter Ueberroth

13. Which team has apparently become more successful than the Sox since the 2005 Series, making them a rival in Chicagoans' minds?

    a. Astros

    b. Braves

    c. Dodgers

    d. Marlins

14. Which of the following names is NOT used to refer to the Cubs-White Sox face-off?

    a. Crosstown Classic

    b. Crosstown Showdown

c. Windy City Knockout

d. Windy City Showdown

15. What's the color of the train line, operated by the Chicago Transit Authority, which stops at both Guaranteed Rate Field and Wrigley field, home of the Cubs on the city's North Side?

    a. Blue Line

    b. Green Line

    c. Lilac Line

    d. Red Line

16. Why did the American League became increasingly popular, and thus a greater rival to the National League, in the 20th century?

    a. Better players

    b. Cheaper alcohol and ticket prices

    c. More high-scoring games

    d. More rain checks

17. What was the first year that the White Sox battled the Cubs when both were respective division leaders?

    a. 1959

    b. 1985

    c. 2005

    d. 2008

18. In 2006, which Cubs catcher blocked A.J. Pierzynski and punched him in the jaw after the latter had scored and slapped the plate?

a. Michael Barrett

b. Aramis Ramírez

c. José Reyes

d. Geovany Soto

19. Ozzie Guillén threw fuel on the fire with various rivals. What word completes this comment about Wrigley: "Because our fans are not stupid like Cubs fans. They know Wrigley Field is just a _____."?

a. bar

b. dump

c. rat hole

d. waste of time

20. For the 2020 season, MLB decided to only allow teams to play teams within their own division and their crossover divisions. Which team is not part of the AL or NL Central?

a. Brewers

b. Cards

c. Diamondbacks

d. Reds

QUIZ ANSWERS

1. C - Billy Koch

2. B - Detroit

3. D - Twins

4. A - The Blackout Game

5. C - Detroit

6. B - 65-63

7. A - True

8. C - 4-3 / 4-3

9. D - A tea party

10. B - 1913

11. D - 2005

12. B - Bud Selig

13. A - Astros

14. C - Windy City Knockout

15. D - Red Line

16. B - Cheaper alcohol and ticket prices

17. D - 2008

18. A - Michael Barrett

19. A - bar

20. C - Diamondbacks

DID YOU KNOW?

1. When Comiskey brought his St. Paul Saints to Chicago, he agreed not to use the city name as part of the team's name. Thus, Charles adopted "the White Stockings" as his first name—the same used by the Cubs from 1876 to 1889.

2. In 1985, an annual "Windy City Classic" charity game between the two Chicago teams was held with the teams alternating stadiums as hosts. It only lasted till '95.

3. After Ozzie Guillén was upset that Jon Garland had "missed" with a retaliation pitch against the Rangers, Tigers first-base coach Andy Van Slyke said he'd have punched the manager if that happened to him. Ozzie's answer: "That's why he's coaching first base, and I'm managing in the big leagues."

4. The White Sox own the historical series over the Twins (originally the Washington Senators): 1,158-1,088 wins.

5. When the Sox squared off against the Tigers in 2000, one innocuous beanball by Chicago's Jim Parque ended up in 11 ejections, 16 suspensions and 24 fines. Keith Foulke also suffered a cut that needed five stitches.

6. From a 2004 court case involving a brawl in the stands of U.S. Cellular Field: "While the two teams (Chicago and Cleveland) maintain a healthy rivalry, this court notes ... the title of arch rival belongs to the reviled Minnesota Twins."

7. The rivalry between the Cubs and White Sox appears to spill over to writers, too. One Bleacher Report article stated: "If you are a baseball fan looking for knowledgeable fans (at Wrigley), good luck. If you look to your left and ask anything, you might get a beer spilled on you."

8. According to another Bleacher Report pundit: "The stage is now set for an exciting new chapter in the Cubs-White Sox rivalry. Their games figure to not only be more frequent, but also more competitive to boot."

9. Rivalry possibly led to Bill Veeck's purchase of the White Sox. He knew about the inter-familial tension within the Comiskey family, so he led the group that bought a controlling interest in the Chicago White Sox in 1959.

10. The Chicago Cubs signed 2013's top international free agent, Eloy Jiménez, a so-called "five-tool" player. But they traded him to the White Sox in 2017 as part of the Jose Quintana deal. Will he lord it over the White Sox's crosstown rivals in the near future?

CONCLUSION

The great White Sox names roll off your tongue: Luke Appling, Shoeless Joe Jackson, Bill Veeck, Buehrle, Ozzie, Nellie, Billy Pierce, Garland, Ted Lyons and Ed Walsh, as well as one of the greatest hitters of all time, Frank "The Big Hurt" Thomas, the muscle man who crushed 521 career homers.

This is it, an amazing collection of White Sox information, statistics, and trivia at your fingertips! Regardless of how you fared on the quizzes, we hope you found this book entertaining, enlightening and educational.

Ideally, you knew many of these details already, but also learned a great deal more about the history of the Chicago White Sox, their players, coaches, managers, and some of the quirky stories surrounding the team, its history and its special ballpark(s). If you got a peek into the colorful details that make being a fan so much more enjoyable, then our mission was accomplished!

The good news is the trivia doesn't have to stop there. Spread the word. Challenge your fellow Chicago fans to see if they can do any better. Share some of the stories with the next generation to help them become White Sox supporters too.

If you're a big enough Chicago White Sox fan, consider creating your own quiz with some of the details you know weren't included here. Then test your friends to see if they can match your knowledge.

The White Sox are one of baseball's most storied franchises with a long history, many stretches of success, and a few that were a bit less so (the 1919 Black Sox Scandal comes to mind). They've had glorious superstars, iconic moments and hilarious tales. Most of all, they have wonderful, passionate fans. Thank you for being one of them. "Appreciate the Game."

Made in the USA
Coppell, TX
18 October 2021